Stewardship Enlistment and Commitment

Dr. Raymond B. Knudsen is the author of

NEW MODELS FOR CREATIVE GIVING
NEW MODELS FOR FINANCING THE LOCAL CHURCH
DEVELOPING DYNAMIC STEWARDSHIP
NEW MODELS FOR CHURCH ADMINISTRATION
MODELS FOR MINISTRY
THE WORKBOOK
  (A companion volume to all of the above)
THE TRINITY

STEWARDSHIP ENLISTMENT AND COMMITMENT

RAYMOND B. KNUDSEN

MOREHOUSE-BARLOW
Wilton

Morehouse-Barlow Co., Inc.
78 Danbury Road
Wilton, Connecticut 06897

ISBN 0-8192-1371-3

Library of Congress Catalog Card Number 85-061218

Printed in the United States of America

2 4 6 8 10 9 7 5 3 1

Dedicated to my ten grandchildren

Anne Mills Knudsen
Silas John Knudsen, Jr.
Bruce Allen Knudsen
Christian Burnes Knudsen
Elizabeth Ann Knudsen
Stephanie Barnett Knudsen
Heidi Lynn Knudsen
Heather Ann Knudsen
David Andrew Semotan
Sarah Ann Semotan

with the prayer that they may continue in the
development of resources
for the family of faith
in the twenty-first century

Contents

Stewardship Enlistment and Commitment

Introduction

In my travels through all fifty states of the United States, as well as in twenty-nine countries in Europe, Asia, and Africa, I have been struck by the failure of the Christian Church to develop adequate resources for its ministry and mission.

The Church has not been neglectful in presenting either the need for or the nature of spiritual commitment. It has, however, completely failed in committing individuals to make a reasonable and proper contribution for the advancement of the Gospel.

The Church has made the need known. One can hardly pick up a religious journal, periodical, report, or tract without discovering funding shortages in every area of the world. Funding is inadequate for educational and medical missions; funding is inadequate for food and shelter costs; funding is inadequate for materials and supplies to develop skills needed by individuals to improve their lives; and funding is inadequate for the construction of churches, chapels, and missions for the preaching of the Gospel. Where there are hospitals, schools, churches, and training laboratories, there is a severe shortage in both staff and materials to further the Gospel in a proper way.

In spite of the tremendous inadequacies, one could survey the whole of Christendom and probably not find a single person who does not know of the need. "The fields are white unto harvest" is the evangel's theme that has universally been heard! However, in the worship of the Church we exaggerate the commitment of persons who worship regularly as well as those who worship only when it is convenient. Most gain the impression that the lack of resources may be attributed to others and not to themselves.

Consider the hymns.

"I surrender all."
"Christ for the world we sing, the world to Christ we bring."
"My Jesus, I love thee. . . ."
"Were the whole realm of nature mine, that were a present far too small, love so amazing, so divine, demands my soul, my life, my all."
"Take my life and let it be, consecrated Lord to thee."

Consider the liturgy.

"Come before His presence with thanksgiving."
"Let us worship through the presentation of tithes and offerings."
"Freely ye have received, freely give."

In the United States, the vast majority of those going to Sunday brunch will leave a larger gratuity for the waiter or waitress than they will have contributed to the Lord's work in the hour of worship. It would be appropriate in our churches if the clergy introduces the offering as the time to accept gratuities or a "small tip." A long-term financial commitment is more representative of the average parishioner's response.

In the sacraments, or ordinances, of the Reformed tradition, there is a pledge made by parents and the parish to raise the child in the "fear and admonition of the Lord" so that the child may mature to a reasonable and responsible Christian life. Almost without exception both parents and the parish fail to take their vows seriously.

In celebration of the Lord's Supper, or Holy Eucharist, the bread and wine are placed upon the altar, or Communion Table, representing the body and blood of our Lord and Savior, Jesus Christ, and we have the gall to place our offerings the very same place with the assumption that our "sacrifice" will be an expression of love and self-giving comparable to the Savior's!

Christianity has failed in the area between making known the need and commitment among those who hold membership in the household of faith. The Church has not been specific about the discipleship of giving. At time we laud the fundamentalist groups (sometimes referred to as "evangelicals") that boast the tithe and fail to realize how inadequate the measure is among those wonderfully blessed with this world's goods. At the same time we praise those who exercise a "faith promise" and emphasize that the stewardship of material resources is a private matter and the decision made in confidence exclusively between the individual and his or her God.

"How much shall I give?"

We've been asked this question often, and leaders among both the clergy and laity have responded, "It is entirely up to you," "This is between you and your God."

The inadequacies in funding persist from week to week, month to month, and year to year. In worship week after week, month after month, and year after year, we boast a commitment inconsistent with the material resources that will give evidence of our faith and meet the need for funding ministry and mission across the nation and around the world.

The needs can be met! The response of Christians can prove responsible! The leadership in Christ's Holy Church must provide for every individual and every family the counsel that will enable them to give witness, in the stewardship of material resources.

This book outlines the means whereby the local church can help the individual and family to mature in faith as responsible stewards of the resources entrusted to their care by their loving heavenly Father. This is not an outline for either a campaign or a financial drive, although there is organization detail to that process. Rather, it is a program whereby individuals consider the opportunity, accept the invitation, and open the door to the greatest blessings life can afford. For as great as the blessings may prove to the household of faith, even greater are the blessings showered upon the individuals and families who respond to the great invitation!

1

Profile of the Individual and the Family Unit

In colonial America, the local church was the center of community life. The clergyman was usually the best, or one of the best, educated persons in the community. He was not only universally known in the community but in turn knew every family and every family member in the community he served.

Society has changed much, especially during the past twenty-five years. Those who belong to a local church now scarcely know the pastor, and the pastor knows very little, in fact almost nothing, of the families holding membership in the parish. Seldom will the group well known by the religious leader exceed 10 percent of the congregation.

If a couple is married, it is possible that the clergy will know only one spouse rather well.

If there are children in the family, it is likely that the clergy will know one or two children, but seldom all. Close relatives (Parents, grandparents, uncles, aunts, etc.) may be a part of the family unit completely unknown to the religious leader. Generally, those members that are known are known only casually.

As a result of limited contacts, the clergy do not know the vocations of members of a family; they have no idea of the education and/or experience of individual family members; they are unaware of the expertise that each individual has in either a vocation or an avocation.

As a result, 90 percent of the persons who join a local church will be inactive by the fifth year of their church memberships simply because they have not become an integral part of the religious family. The tragedy lies in the fact that at the end of the five years they are not even missed. In fact, they are not missed even at the very beginning as early absences occur. If those persons are called upon, it may be in a financial campaign to solicit budget support, and the usual response is that they will either give the same amount as last year or return the response form to the church the next time they attend. Seldom, if ever, is another call made to a parishoner. Most, today, can say that a clergyperson has never been in their home!

The church establishment often proceeds with little concern for the individual or the families. Programs are not based on the need of the parishioners when no one in leadership is knowledgeable of what those needs are. Rather the program of education and worship usually follows traditional concepts that have emerged from past centuries embellished with creative ideas that have worked somewhere else and may work again. If programs succeed, the credit goes to the people. If they do not, the leadership and administration are responsible. Success is accidental when programs are introduced to the parish without research and planning. (We cannot completely fault this form of success, for we can be thankful that from time to time the organized religious family succeeds in meeting the needs of a congregation.)

If we are to meet the needs of a congregation, we simply must know the basic makeup of the parishioners.

Obviously we begin with an address list that provides the name of the family or the family head. If we limit the listing here, however, we will know very little about the family.

If a Mr. _____ is the head of a household, he may be a single person, a widower, or a separated spouse. If it is a Ms. _____ we face the same questions.

What of family members in the household? Is it a couple planning a family or has the nest already emptied? Are there children residing at home and/or children living away from home, either estranged from the parents, away at school, or establishing new homes and families?

Are there other relatives in the family complex? Grandparents, grandchildren, uncles, aunts, nephews, nieces, cousins, or unrelated persons?

What is the age and sex of each family member as well as educational background?

Is there an exceptional person of any age in the family unit? What is his or her situation?

Here in place of simply a name is an identification of the family as a social unit—a unit to share in ministry and a unit to be ministered unto.

Further understanding of a family emerges as we gain information concerning their dwelling place. Does the family reside in a single dwelling, a town house, an apartment, a cooperative, or a condominium? Is the family a tenant or a homeowner? Certain assumptions emerge as we gain understanding of values intrinsic to a person's or family's estate.

Income estimates relative to the value of property are not valid today unless the year when the family took residence is taken into consideration; most of the families who have been making mortgage payments over a period of a decade or more may not be in a position to purchase their residence at the current market value. Actually, the value of property has escalated far more rapidly than personal family income.

Further understanding of the family emerges as we learn of each family member's education, vocation, and avocation. Where is each member employed? Where have they previously worked? How long have they been in their present position? Are they happy or unhappy with their employment? Considering the employment of each family member, what is the take-home pay of each family member in estimated ranges of five thousand dollars? Of each family?

How does each family member relate to the community? Are they members of social and community organizations? Do they support the arts as participants, sponsors, or those who attend? Have they related directly to community needs through leadership or membership positions and/or funding?

Through the years, how has each family member related to the church? What is their experience in the areas of Christian Education? Church and institutional structure? Administration?

What offices have they held? How effective have they been in the religious community as participants in worship and in the organizational life of the institution?

Information limited strictly to a person's or family's present relationship with a church is not adequate. As comprehensive a picture as possible must be gained of the total religious experience from the cradle to the present day. The genius in religious service has often been lost to organizational life and work when the transplant from one communion, or local church, to another simply did not take root. Seldom are all family members equally effective in each local church situation.

Now one needs to consider not only the active life of each person in the organization, but one must come to an understanding of the financial commitment as well. For where the financial commitment is weak, the spiritual health is in jeopardy. A person cannot sustain spiritual health without the exercise of good stewardship over financial resources. Here, far too few will have gained the stature of Christian discipleship.

In every case, an analysis should be made not only of what each individual and family can give but also where each should be in the supporting role of the local church and organized religion. An estimate of contribution is derived from comparing those of like income and family structure, taking as the standard those who have matured in their lives as good stewards of material resources.

Over the past forty-five years I have discerned two things: one, that 80 percent of the funding comes from 20 percent of the people, and two, that the 20 percent of the families who contribute significantly represent a reasonable cross section of 80 percent of the congregation. Accepting these two observations as valid, it is not difficult to place 80 percent of a congregation in a proper level of financial support that would be seen as each assumes a reasonable and proper role in the support of ministry and mission.

If, as a first step, one-half of the 80 percent who are giving only 20 percent of the funding increase their support to the level of those in the top 20 percent, there would be an immediate increase in the local church funding of 160 percent. The local church with a budget of $100,000 would increase their support to fund ministry and mission in the amount of $260,000 in a single year! If the other 40 percent were to make a similar increase, the support would fund ministry and mission by another 160 percent or bring the annual budget of $100,000 per year to the sum of $420,000 per year.

In addition to resources presently untapped in the local church, one family unit is capable of funding ministry and mission in an amount equal to the giving of the total congregation. That increases the budget potential in the example above by another $420,000. At every level of financial support there is one person or family who can contribute as much as forty persons or families combined. Here is another $420,000.

The potential for funding actually stands at $1,260,000! This potential rests with the parish with a current budget of $100,000. The same percentages may be applied to both larger and smaller parishes.

In capital funding the potential is a dollar per dollar match over a period of three years. In the case illustrated the potential for capital funding would total $3,780,000!

Now if the potential for financial development in the local church is so very great, think of the potential that is available in other areas, namely, programs and leadership.

When a comprehensive listing is completed of individuals and families, identifying the types of members and their situations, the doors open for expanding present programs and developing new programs and services to increase substantially the relationships and opportunities that make the local church supremely important to the members of the household of faith.

The tendency among church administrations is to consider programming, as well as potential for programming, simply in terms of the persons presently involved in the church's life and work. As in the area of budget support, we probably are dealing effectively with a limited number in our membership and in many cases truly fewer than 20 percent.

Discovering the situation that prevails among the adult membership, one can begin to see the potential of programs in new ways: for senior adults in terms of men, women, and couples; for parents in terms of single parents, one working spouse, and two working spouses; single young adults in terms of male and female, and those who are seeking companionship as they look toward marriage.

Consider ministry to children and young people as the number and needs emerge from the profiles. Here one gains the exact figure for those who may be considered in any program.

In developing programs, regardless at the age level, remember to consider the multiple needs of individuals ranging from their life and work in the local church to each of their vocations and avocations. The more effectively the local church relates to each person's need, the more meaningful the religious organization will become in the life and work of the individual.

Viewing the membership in terms of needs obviously leads to the question, Who in the world will do all of the work that needs to be done to meet these needs? The profiles that produced the potential for funding and program development will produce the potential leadership as well. The profiles should support two facts: First, the local church has not begun to use the potential leadership that resides in the local parish. Second, few who volunteer services to the local church do so in the area of their greatest expertise. In essence, the local church has the right people in the wrong jobs in many events.

Think of the potential that lodges in every person exercising their expertise in ministry and mission if for only two, three, or four hours each week!

The key to the fulfillment of ministry and mission lies in the profiles. This is truly the right place to begin.

2

The Profiles Task Force

My experience in working with local churches across the nation and around the world has shown that task forces restricted in responsibility can best meet the needs of a program. The broader the portfolio, the less effective the process. When responsibilities are broad, certain portions of the assignment are met, one or two somewhat adequately and some not dealt with at all. However, when the task is sharply defined, the task force functions effectively, and the effort is carried out satisfactorily and in a proper time frame.

Experience further underlines the fact that the most effective task forces are those whose membership is limited to three persons. When a task force consists of more members, they usually meet when three can get together and usually it is not the same three members. If the task force consists of only three members, they tend to meet when all can be present, and the work proceeds with full understanding and cooperation.

When selecting three persons to serve on the Profiles Task Force, it is essential that the three persons meet these criteria:

First, they must be persons capable of keeping information confidential and persons whose integrity and reliability will not be questioned by any member of the congregation. The task they assume is an important one, and they must be able to exercise good judgment and at the same time keep in confidence matters that are often quite personal.

11

Second, the members who serve on the Profiles Task Force must have a broad acquaintanceship in the parish and a good relationship with organizational leaders in both the church and the community. Generally they are persons who have been active not only in their local church but in community organizations as well. As such, they will be able to enlist the cooperation of key leaders in both the church and the community that may be most helpful to the process.

Third, they must be persons who are comfortable with organizing details and capable of delegating responsibilities to those who will assimilate the information for the profiles.

Often an effective Profiles Task Force will consist of a person of mature years who is retired from an administrative post; a woman who has been active in volunteer work and/or Christian education; and a person at life's prime who is involved in community organizations.

To start, the Profiles Task Force should assimilate the names and addresses of all persons enrolled in the membership of the local parish and all of its organizations: choirs, Sunday school classes, youth groups, scout troops, athletic groups, interest groups, and community organizations that meet in the local church.

As the material is assembled, one will notice that a large percentage of families will be listed by individual names lifted from organizational rosters and placed in the family profiles. There will be voids in many cases as not all members of a family relate to the local church. One spouse may belong to the local church and the other to another parish or to no church at all. A high-school youth may be the only member of a family attending a local parish. In some cases the relationship a family has with a church is solely through the children's participation. Even so, each family member is important as gradually we assimilate information concerning the members and related families in a local parish.

As work proceeds, the task force should not limit information to those families where only one or two parents are members of the local church. Include all family members in the family profiles or the profiles will not be adequate to provide the information required to develop resources and administer the organization effectively.

Indices emerge automatically concerning the paticipant. In

some groupings the age will be exact; in some groupings the age will fall into a category such as college age, middle age, or senior citizen; and in some groupings there will be no key to the age factor at all. However, one can estimate the age of the parents of a college-age person as forty-five to fifty-five years of age. If the college-age student is the youngest of four children, one can peg age of the parents at fifty-five years of age plus. Obviously, if children are of preschool age, the parents will generally be under thirty-five years of age.

Generally the information we have suggested gathering so far is the easiest to obtain. Other information is more difficult and time-consuming to gather.

The next step is to identify the vocations of the family members who may be gainfully employed. One spouse may be a department head in a clothing store, the second spouse a school teacher; and a resident sibling a legal secretary. Positions held by individual family members provide a rather effective picture of the family's economic position in terms of annual earnings. One must not assume that annual earnings provide an adequate index to a family's economic condition. Some with modest earnings may have inherited large sums of money and have substantial income from investments. Some with seemingly high income may be in a tight economic condition because of tuition costs, poor health, or adverse conditions in the marketplace. Annual earnings need to be computed against the other factors affecting economic life and security.

The kind of residence a person or family lives in is also of great importance in establishing the profile. Determine the value of the home or apartment, whether members own or are in the process of purchasing a property or whether they occupy a cooperative or condominium.

When considering the value of the residence, it is important to determine the approximate date on which a person or family took occupancy. In this respect we can weigh the inflationary factors against the present value. As previously stated, many would be unable to affort their present residences were they to acquire them at the current market value.

If the value of the residence exceeds the estimated earnings of the family or the individuals, in all likelihood there has been a significant inheritance, or windfall, which has contributed substantially to the family's or individual's economic well-being. Wise investments, too, may have played a significant role in the economic well-being of the family or the individual.

Now we have two indices (income and property) that are helpful in determining the average church family's or individual's potential for giving. However, we must recognize that no persons are likely to elevate their giving from a totally insufficient base to one that complements their faith in Christ in a single step. Therefore the profiles need to include information as to where they are, as a family group and as individuals, in the exercise of Christian stewardship.

If possible, the profiles should include the pledges and records of giving of all members over a period of five years. Did they make a firm commitment in any one, or all five, year(s)? Did they make regular payments toward the commitment or was the obligation met in a single payment? If the obligation was met in a single payment, it is likely they could provide greater support if programmed on a monthly, or quarterly, basis. Did they totally meet their pledge? Or, did they contribute more, or less, than their pledge?

In the course of the preceding five years, consider special offering opportunities. What opportunities did the members take advantage of? To what did they contribute substantially? To what did they contribute modestly? To which opportunities did they make no response whatsover?

In the course of the five years did they make a special gift to their church? Did they fund a memorial? Did they contribute to the memorial fund as an expression of sympathy to members, friends, or neighbors?

Now we need to cross over the threshold from the local church to the community to discover the interest of the members in community organization and development.

One way to make an analysis of giving is by providing postal cards on which members are asked to list the eight organizations to which they have contributed over the last twelve months, as well as the amount. Members may, in addition, list their name and address on the postal card if they choose. However, it is simple to key each card to identify the response.

In the letter accompanying the postal card, the stewardship chairperson can merely say that a survey is being made among the members and friends of the church to determine both the amount and the causes to which they provided funding. In many cases the largest contributions are not made to the local church except in the case of a capital funds drive. Usually the largest gifts are made to colleges and universities, hospitals and community organizations, cultural and civic groups, environmental and social concerns. In many cases, because of payroll deductions or preauthorized giving, individuals will contribute more to the United Way than to their local church. Take note that the major support for all organizations outside the local church will come from the supporting families and members in a local church! Those who attend the local church respond most readily to the funding needs that are made known across the nation and around the world.

If this course is not to be pursued, then I suggest that key leaders in community organizations be invited to go through the profiles and add their input from their involvement with members and friends in supporting the organizations in which they have a common interest. For example, a person who has served as a chairperson or a key leader in a hospital drive or community fund campaign will often be able to provide significant information concerning key potential donors in the local church.

When all of these factors are taken into account, the Profiles Task Force will be able to detemine where the particular family should be on the escalator of financial support. If a person takes a step on an escalator, there is additional progress each step of the way. So also in Christian stewardship. As the individual responds to particular funding needs for ministry and mission, they tend to move in a regular and consistent manner in expanding their sights as well as exercising more responsible stewardship over their material resources.

The Profiles Task Force occupies a significant role in the process. While the profiles may not be complete even when the task force is employed, understanding parish potential will be less than adequate without it.

3

Information and Interpretation

One could very well assume after reading the first two chapters that all we have to do is to learn where the funding potential is in order to gain the resources required for ministry and mission. While it is important to discover where the potential for funding is, and the sums the potential for funding represent, it is not valid to assume that the funding will actually come simply because the potential is there.

If persons are to respond generously and enthusiastically, they must be well informed. A well-informed person will do the right thing. Unless families and individuals are well informed of the opportunity, the need, and what is reasonably expected of them to give, they will not share. Of course, there will be some response but it will be only tokenism in terms of the potential that lies within the members and friends of the local parish.

Perhaps the best place to begin is to inform potential donors about the place of philanthropic giving in the Gospel and interpret the promises of our blessed Savior to those who are good stewards of financial resources. Here the local parish has been remiss in not emphasizing the importance of giving to the individual.

The promises are numerous and actually begin with the Lord's Prayer itself when we are taught to say: "Forgive us our debts, as we forgive our debtors." God's forgiveness of our debts, trespasses, transgressions, and sins are determined by the forgiveness we exercise toward others.

In the same vein our Lord states: "Give and it shall be given unto you. Full measure, pressed down and shaken together. For the measure you give is the measure you shall receive." The individual establishes the measure of God's gifts. "The measure you give is the measure you will receive."

Other than reciting the biblical promises, how can these truths be truly transmitted to the members and friends in the local parish? Actually it takes the personal witness of persons who have experienced the grace of God through their own philanthropic orientation. In every parish there are persons young and old, couples establishing their lives and families, and some nearing the end of their lives, who have modeled their life to the spiritual promises of good stewardship. Their experiences can be shared with those who continue to question the goodness of God and His faithfulness in keeping His promises. While individual benevolence matters greatly to the religious institution, the greater blessing is upon the donor. The Gospel portrays this beyond the shadow of a doubt.

In addition to drawing on God's word and personal testimony to educate people about stewardship, we must present funding needs for ministry and mission in terms of program. Most budgets are drawn up in terms of supporting an institution. Heat and light, repair and maintenance, materials and supplies, staff and equipment. There is little incentive to give when the end result of our giving is to preserve an institution. Actually the institution should be the vehicle for *implementing* the program.

Let us consider a number of areas.

Christian education. A primary function of the local church is to educate persons of all ages in the Christian faith. In a sense this is evangelism too. An individual is converted to Christianity when the person learns about the faith and the meaning of the faith to the individual for spiritual growth and life. Education is needed for both those without the household of faith who are to come to a knowledge of our Lord and Savior, Jesus Christ, and those who are within the household of faith that they may grow in faith and knowledge.

Traditionally we have thought of evangelism for those without the household of faith as being met through the "communicant's class," and the "confirmation class." Yet, these classes are truly not adequate in meeting this objective as in most cases they are structured to assist those who are already a part of the Christian ideology or environment, generally the spouses, children, and family members of the believers.

Churches need a broader program of education. I believe that classes at nonsectarian colleges and universities in Christian ethics, Old Testament, New Testament, and comparative religion come closest to the mission of the local church in reaching those persons who have not been raised in church-related families or in the environment of organized religion. If the peoples of the world are to be brought to Jesus Christ, a significant portion of a church's program must be in educating those persons who are indeed beyond the fringe of the religious, or Christian, constituency.

So often the major portion of the local church's funding to this end has been to fund the institutions that are engaged in such ministries beyond the walls of the local church. We fund national missions, foreign missions, colleges, and seminaries both at home and abroad. The greatest areas for evangelical concern are in the area of each local parish. In the United States, local churches tend to weaken from generation to generation in a mobile society, and the strength of the institution in the future depends upon an aggressive and vital evangelism program. However, the purpose of evangelism is not to preserve the institution! Rather, it is to meet the mandates of the Gospel: "Go ye therefore and teach all nations, baptizing them in the name of the Father, and of the Son, and of the Holy Ghost. Teaching them to observe all things which I have commanded you." As long as there is a single person beyond the redemptive society, the local church's primary mission is not fulfilled.

While perhaps incorporated in the field of evangelism, the Christian education of children, youths, young adults, and adults will hardly be covered by the inquirer's class, communicant's class, and confirmation class. However, education should be much broader and include the Sunday school, the vacation church school, Bible study classes, Weekday education, youth groups, choirs, officers' training, and continuing education in every aspect of religious orientation and instruction. Women's organizations and men's organizations in the parish should be included as well.

A program for evangelism and Christian education are the first items in the program budget for which a cost analysis of the institution's life and work can be made. Calculate the costs of each in terms of

salaries/personnel
space/maintenance and preservation
materials and supplies
equipment

In establishing the program budget we often err in not including all our costs. For example, in budgeting personnel for education and evangelism a large church would tend to include only the salaries of the minister of evangelism and the director of Christian education. Yet every staff person including those providing administration and custodial services, will be spending a portion of their time for each and every aspect of the local church's life and work. The portion of time given to the function should be identified under the particular cost of the life and work of the institution.

A further illustration may be helpful. Usually the minister of music, the choir director, and the organist have their salaries computed under the area of worship, but actually a far greater portion of their time is spent in Christian education relative to the mission of the church than at the worship service. Their services must be computed as a part of the Christian education program as well as a part of the worship program.

This brings us next in the program budget to worship.

In most churches the sanctuary, represents the greatest capital outlay of the institution. Yet, of all of the areas in a local parish it is probably the most underutilized area in the church's physical plant. Probably few sanctuaries are used more than 150 hours per year at the most, which computes to only six and one-fourth days of time. When one is confronted by this fact, there is reason to consider the dimension of church programs to determine where greater services may be provided to utilize more adequately the costliest facility in the institution. For example, if the sanctuary was used as a music studio for organ instruction and practice, this would add as many as 450 hours in utilization of the facility. If the sanctuary was used for recitals, concerts, lectures, and drama, it is likely that another 300 hours could be added to the utilization of the facility in the course of a year. Prorating costs to the institution in terms of the two areas just described reduces the cost of the sanctuary for worship by 84 percent!

The utilization of the space in the sanctuary is a perfect illustration of the utilization of the facilities as well.

In many local churches the educational facilities are not limited to Sunday morning usage as for Sunday school. It is not unusual to discover that church facilities are used by voluntary organizations: scouts, Alcoholics Anonymous, etc. While these are important services that a parish may provide, they cost the church money in terms of staff and facilities. Consider these costs as a part of the community service and outreach budget but, at the same time, consider the programs in which the local church may be engaged as a means of service as well as a means of recovering the operational costs of the institution.

Programs that fall into this category could include nursery and preschool services, senior day-care services, latchkey programs, and organized classes in arts, crafts, literature, and computer science. A compilation of services must be made by each local church to determine the actual needs for programming in each area. In most cases a local church will determine a program in terms of what some other parish has done. Actually the needs of one parish may be quite different from the needs of another. One parish may try to establish a strong program for high-school youths when there are too few young people in the community for a successful effort. At the same time, another parish may try to develop an extensive program for senior citizens and discover that the number eligible for such a program simply no longer resides in the area. It is a misadventure to endeavor to transplant a program from one geographical location to another. It simply does not work. Programs must emerge from the needs that exist in each community, and if programs do not meet the need, not only will they falter but they will actually fail.

With the rising divorce rate and the number of single parents who choose not to marry increasing, many individuals must rely on services for the care of children during the hours when they are gainfully employed. If there is no child care, many parents cannot work. The budgets of single-parent families are generally quite limited, and they can often pay only a modest fee for child care.

This imposes a rather serious limit on the organizations providing child-care services. If the fee exceeds the single-parent's funding potential, the parent will simply become, or remain, unemployed and depend on support from the government for public assistance.

Now there are many churches that simply cannot provide child-care services because of inadequate facilities. There will be many members of a church with adequate facilities who do not believe that this is a reasonable and responsible mission opportunity. I, personally, believe that it is. However, I do believe that many churches err in providing a custodial and landlord service to privately operated child-care services. If the program is in the local church, it should be administered and operated as a program of the local church, and in this respect it should be an instrument for evangelism to families.

Child-care services are also needed by the majority of families in the United States today inasmuch as both spouses are gainfully employed. While there is a strong emphasis on fathers and mothers caring for children, work schedules are such that when both parents are gainfully employed it is essential that child care be available at least a part of the time.

There are those parents who are anxious that their child have a preschool experience because they believe that a child with this opportunity will mature more rapidly in Christian and social graces. For these families, child-care services provide a life-enrichment opportunity.

Community service and outreach does not stop here. Let us go to the other end of the spectrum and consider the services that should be provided to mature persons or senior citizens.

First among the needs of senior citizens in our society is a service to assist them in handling responsibilities that become more difficult with time to manage. Forms for health services, relating to both government programs (Medicare and Medicaid) and to self-insuring programs that many persons have in addition to the governmental provisions, are one example. Many individuals come to a time in life when they simply cannot handle these details, and they are in need of assistance. The local church can do much to meet this need by establishing a cadre of capable persons who will provide the service on a graduated-fee basis. It is not essential that these services be done gratuitously. In fact, many who need the services simply will not use them unless they can pay a fee for services rendered.

A second important need that has emerged among senior citizens is a senior day-care service. Just as preschool children are in need of day care, so are parents, grandparents, and other dependent seniors living with a sibling, relative, or friend. They require a custodial type of service during the working hours of those gainfully employed in the household. These persons need supervision in terms of activities, medication, and rest periods. They are persons who simply cannot be left alone.

Regulations placed upon local churches providing these services are rather strict, and it is essential that they be fully met. It is equally important that the local church meet the need when it exists. The need will progressively increase because of the advancing age of persons in the United States today. The number of senior citizens in proportion to the population will continue to gain throughout the foreseeable future.

Personal estate planning and consultation in financial management are other important services that may well be provided on a graduated-fee basis. Generally, among senior couples, one spouse will handle financial affairs. At the death of a spouse, the surviving spouse is often completely unprepared and ill equipped to assume the responsibility of their personal finances without assistance. In large estates this is not a problem, for there are many persons in the financial, banking, and investment fields, as well as legal counsel, who will provide the services; in most cases they will have been engaged far in advance to the time the first spouse dies. Many will have such modest resources that they will not gain the consideration and counsel they require from the professional person. Here the local church may provide a unique and important service as the exercise of the stewardship of material resources is implemented by qualified persons serving through the local parish.

A fourth service relates to travel and interest groups. When I first became a member of the board of directors for Presbyterian Senior Services in New York City, the organization was offering senior citizens the opportunity to share in bus trips on a one day or two day schedule. One trip was scheduled to Colonial Williamsburg and another to New England in the fall of the year. The primary purpose was to provide economical travel for persons of modest means. I emphasized to the board that it was essential that the needs of persons with greater financial resources be met as well as those with modest resources. A trip was offered to England, Scotland, and Wales, and more than forty persons signed up for the first scheduled opportunity. A rather extensive travel program is being developed by the organization, and it is likely that substantial bequests will come in the course of the next quarter century because of this service to people with considerable financial resources. This type of opportunity can be offered by the local parish, and in some cases a group of local churches could go together. These opportunities, of course, will occupy little time for the participant in terms of a year, or years, but provide much joy in terms of anticipation and recollection.

Interest groups, as well as travel groups, need to be encouraged. Interests may include literature, science, the arts, and all types of handicrafts. Enrollment fees may be established for each group in order that the financial needs of the organization be met on a fair share basis.

There is a broad area of concerns and needs that exists among teenagers, young adults, and those at life's prime. In many cases the needs will be the same. Recreational opportunities—not in terms of entertainment, but recreation as the re-creation of the individual through broadening acquaintanceship, experience, and knowledge—will constitute a sizable program.

Our society consists of lonely persons, and individuals cannot live whole lives without relationships with their peers as well as with those of diverse interests and experience. I know of no organization that provides as great an opportunity for broad experience in interpersonal relationships as the local church. Chairpersons of the boards of corporations mix with the custodial staff in public schools, and there is no feeling of embarrassment on the part of the one or insufficiency on the part of the other. Those with earned doctorates mingle with those who have only an elementary education, and again there is a sense of parity between them. Programs must be developed to enhance these opportunities. These programs will basically be for fellowship.

In formal education we have failed by and large to train individuals in the forms of physical recreation that one may engage in by oneself. Physical education usually consists of interschool or intramural team activities on the gridiron, diamond, or court. These opportunities conclude with graduation.

The local church can well meet the need of individuals as teams are organized in many sports for both male and female participants, as well as mixed teams, at the different age levels.

Services may be provided by scheduling games of golf, handball, tennis, for those who are apt to share in this type opportunity. More than physical activity takes place, for no person can engage in these activities without broadening social relationships with new acquaintances in the household of faith.

A third need is that of knowledge, and there are dozens of opportunities for the local church to assist individuals not only in the study of the Scriptures and the Christian faith but in the individual's total relationship to life. Study groups may be formed to discuss parenting, adjusting to life as a single parent, understanding the adolescent, facing problems in marriage and family life, financial management, the arts and science.

As groups are developed, as well as activities scheduled, the program budget is expanded to include the cost of the programs. Here, too, the budget should be computed in terms of

salaries/personnel
space/maintenance and preservation
materials and supplies
equipment

There is another aspect that must be considered in the program budget of the local church and that is the broader mission of the church in terms of the universal witness. In some locations this will be known as benevolences; in some communions as apportionments; and in still other parishes as a missions budget.

Few parishes properly budget for this. Not only do they contribute too little to the universal witness, but they actually do not compute the cost of the contributions they make. Generally a local church will set aside a portion of the budget for mission and say, "This is what we give!" And, it is indeed the sum that is sent to the mission boards. However, administrations fail to compute the cost of developing and administering mission funds—as much as an additional 25 percent of the mission remittance. Think of mailings, postage, bookkeeping as well as materials and supplies. The funds could not be available without these supporting services.

Then, too, in the connectional system; realize that ordained staff persons will fill demands by the judicatory averaging 20 percent of their time. About four days each month will be given to the work of the denomination, as well as to ecumenical services; this time needs to be computed in the budget, for it is a significant and substantial contribution. The connectional system could not exist without it.

With the universal witness one must consider the cost of staff, space and travel needs, and materials and supplies that are essential to the funding and services. Here, too, the program budget breaks down into four groupings:

salaries/personnel
space/maintenance and preservation
materials and supplies
equipment

The Information and Interpretation Task Force has the responsibility of assisting in the development of the program budget, especially in providing an understanding of the mission and ministry of the local church as provided through the program budget.

When the process first begins, the members may be appalled at the voids that exist in meeting the program needs of a congregation in the average local church. Few have begun to scratch the surface of program potential in most parishes.

It will take a great deal of time to develop the program budget, and such a budget should be in place three months before the stewardship enlistment and commitment program is undertaken.

Now there are other things that the Information and Interpretation Task Force must consider with the administrative board before a twelve-month information and interpretation process is launched. Let us consider at least a few.

First, the administrative board should seek pledges on a monthly, rather than a weekly, basis. It is unfortunate that the local church seems locked into funding processes that relate to a weekly offering in a society that no longer budgets by the week. By and large the church moved from an annual funding base when society became monetarily oriented. With the industrial revolution the weekly payday became the norm, and gradually the local church developed an envelope system that accommodated that change. Now, however, in a society that budgets on a monthly basis it is expected that announced intentions for giving be made on a monthly basis as well. In the present system people tend to become overly impressed by what they give, not because they give much, but because they give often. Sound fiscal processes can emerge in the local chuch instantly when funding is on a regularly monthly basis.

Second, the administrative board should approve the enlistment of announced intentions for giving on a two and one-half year, ten-quarter, basis. It is not practical for a local church to seek financial commitments annually, and it is difficult not only to recruit the leadership in an annual process but to generate the interest and enthusiasm that is essential to the process. Many become overly impressed with the local church's emphasis on financial need and giving because as many as six to eight weeks each year may be given to the developmental process in funding the annual budget.

Then, too, we need to realize that if the financial emphasis is scheduled each fall it comes at a time when persons are feeling greatly burdened. There are increased costs in living through the winter months, and wage earners, and/or those on fixed incomes, have a greater difficulty in elevating their sights for giving in the fall of the year when the costs of utilities, clothing, and festivities are the greatest of the year. People will generally respond to overtures for increased funding more substantially in the spring than in the fall. The ten-quarter commitment process makes this possible once in each five years.

Those persons whose incentive for giving is enhanced by taxation will respond most generously in the fall of the year. Supporting evidence has found that 60 percent of the money that is given to eleemosynary (charitable) organizations flow from donor coffers to those of institutions between the tenth day of December and the sixth day of January each year. These persons will increase their giving most readily when the overtures are made for Thanksgiving and year-end giving.

This does not mean that a local church will be locked into a two and one-half year, or ten-quarter, budgeting process. Actually budgeting should be on an annual basis. However, as one enters the budget period for the year in which the stewardship enlistment takes place in the spring, a modified budget should be prepared by the administration board for the second six-month period in that particular year.

Opportunity should also be given to each person to adjust their giving on an annual basis even in the ten-quarter commitment process. This may be done by letter, and one of several forms may invite individual consideration of the stewardship opportunity.

One form would provide opportunity for individuals to check a 5, 10, 15 percent or other increment. For a fall effort the letter and response form should be mailed early in October. The response form should state that if the form is not returned to the church, or church office, by the tenth day of November, the local support level for ministry and mission will be adjusted to a 5 percent increase; when the local church is at a more comfortable economic level, the response form can state that if the form is not returned to the church, or church office, by 10 November the present level of support will be anticipated for budget planning.

The response to this approach has been excellent where it has been implemented across the nation and around the world. The process should be used each year except when there has been a spring commitment process. That commitment should be considered valid for an eighteen month period.

While I have suggested that nonresponse may be computed as merely sustaining support through an ensuing period, and many churches elect this option, I strongly advise against it. I believe we should not permit members and friends in a congregation to assume that we believe that support level of the average communicant to be consistent with their Christian witness. Such a procedure would imply that their giving is an adequate expression of their faith. This would be true of only a very very few.

Third, the administrative board should adopt AUTOGIVE as an opportunity for members and friends to preauthorize contributions to the local church through automatic withdrawals against checking accounts on a regular basis. This provides for giving on a monthly basis. At the same time, the local parish is assured of substantial support through the twelve months of each year. As holidays, vacations, illnesses, and adverse weather conditions affect church attendance and regular support through the twelve months of the year, AUTOGIVE provides the means whereby financial support may be permanently assured as funds flow from donors' accounts to that of the local church regularly.

This system has been developed by the National Consultation on Financial Development, and a local church may enroll at a modest fee of fifty dollars if the budget is under $100,000 per year. The larger parishes will be required to pay $100. In each event this is a one-time cost.

In addition, as donors sign up, there will be a one-time charge to the local church of fifty cents per donor to program the authorization into the system of the Automatic Clearinghouse Association, which is responsible for moving the funding from any donor's account in any commercial bank (and savings banks and credit unions in many instances) in the United States to the account of the local church. Funds are available for expenditure by the local church treasurer on the day of transfer!

The monthly fee is twenty cents per transaction with a minimum fee for the local church of one dollar per month. One hundred transactions per month would cost just twenty dollars.

Reports are generated by the National Consultation on Financial Development for each participating local church, and the cost of the reports is incorporated in the transaction fee.

Each month the local church will receive a Payments Journal listing all of the donor's names, their bank account numbers, the sum debited each donor's account, and the sum credited to the local church's checking account. The local church may elect payments from donors on the fifth or twentieth day of each month. If the selected day falls on a holiday or Sunday, funds transfer the first business day thereafter, and expenditures may be made from the local church's account that very day.

Each month the local chruch will receive a File Maintenance Journal showing the additions, deletions, or changes in sums being transferred as per donor's authorization. This report provides verification of instructions the local church has given to the National Consultation on Financial Development relative to their donors.

In the event there is an incomplete transaction due to insufficient funds or closing of an account, the funding for the local church is taken from a trust account established by the National Consultation on Financial Development in United Jersey Bank, and deficiencies are met for the particular date from the funds in trust. As a result, a third report, the Uncollected Payments Journal, is sent to the local church. This is a notification of the sums that will be debited from the next transfer of funds to replenish the loan from the trust account. The local church may contact the donor to make an adjustment in the original commitment or correct the incomplete transaction.

It is unlikely that any local church will have a strong financial base for the future without the utilization of a preauthorized funding procedure, which assures a regular and substantial income to the organization.

One should not expect that every family or individual will participate in the AUTOGIVE process. Many will welcome the opportunity, but a large group simply will not respond to such an overture at the present time. However, as we near the conclusion of the check-writing period in American history, and the banking procedures of our time, the local church will have few viable alternatives.

A certain reluctance to give will be evident at the Sunday offering. Looking at a congregation during the worship service, one will be amazed to see how many persons presently do not share in the offering procedure. In fact, only 16 percent of the offering envelopes manufactured in the United States get to church, and local churches have emphasized the importance of this procedure for over a half a century.

Now, if responding affirmatively to the four opportunities outlined above, the administrative board will have approved the following:

1. The program budget
2. Announced intentions for giving on a monthly basis
3. The institution of the ten-quarter commitment period
4. The opportunity for individual donors to authorize regular monthly support through AUTOGIVE

Based on the assumption that an informed people will do the right thing, it is important that enough time be given to the Information and Interpretation Task Force to do its task well.

If the stewardship enlistment and commitment process is to take place in the September to November time segment, the process should begin the first week in September. If the schedule calls for a spring program with new commitments implemented on 1 July, the program should be scheduled over a twelve week period preceding, and including, the third Sunday in May.

In the course of the twelve week period I would suggest that three letters be mailed to the constituency as a way of informing members and friends about the process and the objective.

The first letter, on personal stationery, carries the signature of a person not presently on the board, but one deeply involved in the administrative process through the years and greatly respected among the members and friends. The purpose of the letter is to introduce the ten-quarter commitment process, AUTOGIVE, and the advantages of these unique and progressive ideas. The writer emphasizes his or her personal support of the process.

The second letter, on stationery prepared for the stewardship enlistment and commitment process, carries the signature of the chairperson of the stewardship effort. The chairperson outlines at length the procedures and objectives of announced intentions and gives the time when overtures will be presented to the constituency or when announced intentions should be made. This letter should be mailed in the fifth week of the twelve week schedule.

The third letter should be on regular church stationery and mailed with the signature of the senior clergyperson. This letter should deal with the theological aspects of giving, as well as the importance of individual funding for ministry and mission through the local church. This letter should be mailed in the tenth week of the twelve week period.

Now there are four additional letters that need to be mailed at the time of stewardship enlistment and commitment.

The first is a letter on the stationery of the stewardship enlistment and commitment effort—with the signature of the chairperson—written to those who will not receive a personal visit. The gist of the letter is that it is not possible to visit all families or individuals this year, and therefore they are invited to announce their intentions for giving by mail or by placing the response form in the offering plate. It should be emphasized in the letter, as well as on the response form, that if a personal visit is desired, persons should retain the card with the promise that if the card, or response form, is not received someone will call.

A second letter should be prepared on personal stationery, mailed with the signature of a donor of nonrecord (nonpledging member), and addressed to donors of nonrecord (nonpledging members). The writer of the letter and the person receiving the letter have something in common—neither has pledged in the past. Now long-range planning (over two and one-half years) will require a rather firm estimate of support, and the writer is presenting an overture to donors of nonrecord to indicate what their giving intentions will be in funding ministry and mission in the local parish on a monthly basis.

A third letter should be prepared on personal stationery and mailed with the signature of a nonresident member and addressed to nonresident members. The letter conveys the importance of the church's role for members, whether they reside in the local community or across the state and nation. This continued ministry requires support, and it is appropriate that an item in the budget be identified for funding by nonresident members. A response form needs to be included in this mailing as in all other letters described in this section.

A fourth letter should be prepared on personal stationery and mailed with the signature of an alumnus (former member) and addressed to all alumni (former members). For many persons active in numerous parishes in the course of their spiritual lives the most significant relationship they will ever have with a local parish will be the relationship they have had with your parish. And, in many cases, the time in which they were active in your parish will have been a period when their resources were most limited. Many alumni will be in a better financial position to fund the local church during the time of their alumni relationship rather than the time of their active resident membership.

A fifth letter should go out with the signature of a nonmember friend of the parish. This letter should be on personal stationery and addressed to all nonmember friends of the local church. The writer should emphasize the cordiality of the parish, their willingness to include friends in projects and programs, and the opportunity for friends to share in the financial support of the local church even though they are not members of the parish and may well be affiliated with other churches in the same city or area.

A sixth letter should be sent with the signature of a community business person on business stationery and addressed to the business community in the area. It should outline the community services provided by the local church to the area and the opportunity for the business community to respond with financial support for those deserving community services.

In each event it is important to select an appropriate individual to sign the letter. Wherever possible the person should have strong name recognition in the church or community, be well respected, and bring both honor and integrity to the process.

Short, and to the point, releases should be included in the Sunday bulletins or programs. Over the period of twelve weeks the following themes should be presented:

1. An indication of Giving. This is not a pledge but an opportunity to suggest the measure of financial support that a family or individual will provide each month beginning at the established date of either 1 January or 1 July.

2. Announced intentions on a monthly basis. Because we no longer live in a society that budgets by the week, it is important that funding for ministry and mission be budgeted on a monthly basis as well. Donors may make weekly, monthly, quarterly, semi-annual, or annual payments, but both the church's budget and the donors' response shoud be announced on a monthly basis.

3. AUTOGIVE. It is important for families or individuals to provide preauthorization of their financial support to the local church on a regular monthly basis to assure that adequate funding for ministry and mission will be available year round.

4. Regular support. Irregular attendance and adverse weather conditions prove a threat to the financial integrity of the organization. Therefore it is essential that support be provided regularly over the year. The emphasis may be on the use of weekly offering envelopes and the opportunity for preauthorized giving through AUTOGIVE.

5. Inadequate support. Weekly support leads to an erroneous assumption that support is generous because of the frequency of the gift. Many donors generally assume that they are giving generously when they are not. Donors should be made aware of this wrong assumption.

6. Sacrificial giving. Discuss funding ministry and mission as emphasized in the liturgy, sacraments, and importance of public worship.

7. Christian education. Discuss funding ministry and mission through Christian education and the importance of adequate funding for making known the tenets of the Gospel through the various projects and programs provided by the local church.

8. Community service and outreach. Discuss funding ministry and mission through community service and outreach, elaborating on the projects and programs of the local church.

9. Benevolences. Discuss funding ministry and mission through the denomination, ecumenical organizations, and direct support across the nation and around the world to worthy projects. Emphasize educational and medical missions, as well as the ministries sustained for those in economically and socially deprived areas.

10. Human development. Discuss funding ministry and mission through the denomination, ecumenical organizations, and direct support around the world with particular emphasis on projects and programs relating to the developing countries and third world needs.

11. Individual commitment. Emphasize the importance of individual commitment to fund ministry and mission. One cannot risk adequate funding for ministry and mission to others. Each must assume a proper response in terms of the Divine Imperative.

12. God's blessings. Discuss the promises of God to those who are generous and the blessings that will come to those who exercise good stewardship over their material resources as philanthropic persons. Blessings do indeed come to those who give.

Over the course of the twelve months, there should be one article in each of the three months in the parish newsletter whether it is published weekly, biweekly or monthly.

The first article should provide a complete overview of the stewardship enlistment and commitment program, the process, and the opportunities.

The second article should give an understanding of the program that the parish is funding through the stewardship enlistment and commitment process. It would be well if a copy of the program budget could be included with the article. Emphasize the program, rather than the institution, which is being funded by the financial intentions and support of the constituency.

The third newsletter article should focus on the theological aspects of Christian stewardship and the importance of the individual's response as a member of the church, as a disciple of Christ, and as a participant in the Christian witness.

At least every other Sunday there should be information included in the worship and educational experience of the parish. This may include personal witness concerning love for Christ's Church, blessings that have come to the individual through support of Christ's Church, and personal reports from those who have seen the church at work in unusual, as well as distant, places. Personal testimony will carry much weight when it is sincere, honest, and brief, as well as to the point. Personal witness should come from a good cross section of the parish in terms of age, sex, and vocational experience.

The task of the Information and Interpretation Task Force should not be limited to the process described here. Every opportunity for use of the public media, local newspapers, radio and television stations, as well as community periodicals, should be utilized as much as possible. Items presented to them for coverage must be attractively packaged and truly newsworthy. If they are not attractive and interesting to the media and the public, it is time to examine both the program and releases to make certain that they are worthy and will prove of real interest and importance to the members and friends in the local church.

During my years in the pastoral ministry, I sent to the press on Saturday a key statement from my Sunday morning sermon for publication on Monday. It was a good discipline, for I believed that if I could not produce one thought that would be newsworthy to the press, I would probably not be able to present an effective message to my congregation. It was most effective!

In reality, the message is the Gospel, and the meaning of that word is always: "Good News!"

4

Selecting Members for the Information and Interpretation Task Force

We have suggested from the start that task forces should consist of three persons. It will be expedient and necessary, of course, to include more than three persons in the information and interpretation process, but the decision making and responsibility should lodge with no more than three persons.

What criteria may be used to determine the type of person to serve on the Information and Interpretation Task Force? Let us consider the three types of persons who would be suitable.

One person should be a good communicator of the written word, a person who can put into words the ideas and objectives that must be shared with the members and friends of the local church. Generally this type of person will have considerable writing experience, an education in writing, or an English degree.

A second person will be the type who is good in public relations and can gain the attention of those who must hear the message or communicate the same. This person should have no difficulty approaching personnel at a newspaper, radio, or television station. This person may be employed in advertising or public relations, or the person may simply show a flair for such work.

A third person would be the type who is artistically inclined and could well serve the information and interpretation process making illustrations, posters, graphs, and pictures.

It must be remembered that the task force members are not selected just to serve the stewardship enlistment and commitment process over a period of twelve weeks. Actually they are to form a permanent body in the local church responsible for interpreting the ministry and mission of the local church on a regular basis. While funding and the development of financial resources are important to the program, even more important is an understanding of the mission the local church is engaged in as a unique institution in the world today.

Informed people will do the right thing! If members and friends have a full understanding of the church's ministry and mission, the need for funding, and what is reasonably expected of each of them as potential donors, the funding needs will be met, as well as the other needs, for personnel and services to carry out the mission at the local level.

5

The Stewardship Enlistment
and Commitment Task Force

The Stewardship Enlistment and Commitment Task Force has two basic responsibilities. First, it has the responsibility to enlist and train those persons who will serve as counselors, meeting with prospective donors, outlining the need for funding ministry and mission, and considering with the potential donors the portion of the projects and programs they may consider funding. Second, the Stewardship Enlistment and Commitment Task Force has the responsibility of coordinating the overtures presented to prospective donors and following through on the visits of the counselors. The task force makes certain that the calls have been made and the results recorded with the financial secretary for establishing the financial base.

Basically, organized religion has done a poor and inadequate job in making financial overtures to the members and friends of a local church. In many cases the opportunity has been presented in general terms by a clergyperson or layperson during a service of worship. In other cases the overture is made through a mail appeal. At times the appeal is a combination of the two, and individuals are encouraged to respond to the pulpit and/or mail appeal; in addition people are recruited to push doorbells and pick up cards from those persons who have not responded.

The Stewardship Enlistment and Commitment Task Force should begin the process by recruiting and training individuals to present overtures for funding to individuals and families on a one-to-one basis. Each counselor should be expected to make four calls. The training process will then be directed toward making the counselor knowledgeable of the task, comfortable with the responsibility, and eager to present the overture to four individuals or families.

Needless to say the task is not for everyone, and it is not a task that every individual can do well. It is a task that a great number can do well with training providing they are good conversationalists, can communicate well, and are sincere in the task they have assumed for the local church.

If 400 visits are to be made and the services of 100 persons enlisted as counselors for training, it may be difficult to recruit 100 persons capable of good conversation, effective communication, and visible sincerity. If only two of the qualities are to be met, it would be better that conversation or communication be lacking rather than sincerity. Sincerity will not be enough, of course, if the individual is not capable of conversation or communication. Most people will overlook a person's weaknesses if they are sincere. If a person is not sincere, good conversation and communication will be inadequate in any situation.

What constitutes good and adequate training for the counselors?

First, I recommend that the training include a full explanation of the process, the programs that are to be funded, and the funding need. Each person should be knowledgeable about the institution, the staff, the program, and the new directions for ministry and mission. A counselor should be able to answer questions relative to the life and work of the institution. In some cases, an answer will have to be researched, but information of general interest should be readily available from the counselor and said in a direct and forthright manner. General information includes the budget, the financial resources of the institution, and present funding needs. Included as well are projected funding needs for the future in the event that adequate funding is not included in the annual budget to meet the need for repairs and improvements on an accrual basis. In addition, the counselor should be able to answer questions concerning the staff, the facilities, and assets and liabilities of the institution.

It is especially important for the counselor to be well informed about new projects and programs as well as those aspects of the church's life for which there is reason to be grateful. In addition,

where there has been a cut in programs, a recession in opportunities, or a marked decline in participation, it is essential that
adequate explanations are available. In some cases programs are
reduced or eliminated simply because there is no longer a demand
for them. In other cases there is not adequate leadership. In still
other cases, the institution does not have the means in terms of
facilities, resources, or personnel to sustain programs. In any event,
answers should be provided for the full understanding of the
potential donor.

The counselor also needs to have a profile as complete as
possible of the prospective donor(s) and the relationship to the
local parish. Is the person or family deeply involved, or do they
only have a casual interest in the organization? Have they been
generous in the funding of ministry and mission, or are they only
token givers? Do they have a keen commitment to the Christian
faith, or is their church relationship only a way to gain accepta-
bility in the community?

Regardless of the financial commitment that results from the
counseling session or visit, the interest and commitment of the prospective donor or family should be enhanced as a result of the
opportunity. Hopefully, a friendship will result that will last
through the years.

While the immediate objective is financial support for ministry
and mission, we must realize that the effectiveness of the process
cannot be determined by the response. In some cases there may be
no immediate response whatsoever. In somes cases the fruit
resulting from the call for the local church may not be known for
months or years. Few calls will be fruitless. Most calls will result in
support, an increased financial commitment, in the long term.
Some results will not be of a type that may be measured at all. A
greater understanding of Christ's work through the local church, a
more meaningful relationship in the fellowship of the believers,
and a stronger relationship to the Christian mission may be gained
from a call. Indeed, in some respects, these may be of greater
importance than the financial commitment.

In many cases counselors may prefer making visits in teams.
They may acknowledge a hesitancy to make calls alone and lack
confidence in their ability to represent the process well. When two
such persons meet a prospective donor the hesitation of the two, or

of one, transfers to the prospective donor; any apprehension limits the effectiveness of the visit. Therefore it is important that all counselors be fully trained, that they gain confidence in their ability to conduct a good visit, and that their personal witness results in affirmative action.

There are times when two or more persons should seek a donation together. These include:

1. The solicitation of a challenge grant for matching funds from a major potential donor. The pastor, the chairperson of the board, and the chairperson of the stewardship enlistment and commitment program should meet with prospective donors to emphasize the need, the process whereby the need is to be met, and the importance of their generous financial support in providing a challenge grant to the parish.

2. An overture for a gift of real estate or personal property that is needed and considered of great value to the institution. In this event the pastor, the chairperson of the board of trustees, and the treasurer may well share in the presentation of the overture.

3. The development of a major gift as a memorial. In this event the clergyperson and the chairperson of the board may well present the opportunity to the prospective donor in concert with a representative of the Memorials Task Force.

When and where should such calls be made? Certainly an appointment should be established at the convenience of the prospective donor. If it is not possible that the visit take place in the donor's residence or office, select a place where a table may be shared in privacy—a country club, a hotel, or a restaurant of a quality consistent with the size of the gift being sought. It is most important that the tab be picked up by the official representing the institution. In no case should the prospective donor be permitted to pick up the tab unless he or she is the host or hostess for the event. Because of a heavy schedule, a prospective donor may prefer to invite the counselor to his or her club or office where the meal is ordered or arranged by the prospective donor and must be placed on an account. At times like these it is advantageous for a counselor to accommodate the prospective donor.

When more than one person is to present the overture, establish the game plan prior to the visit. The introduction should be made by the person who is most familiar to the prospective donor. If none are familiar to the donor, the conversation should begin with the clergyperson or the head of the institution. The need should be outlined by the person representing the responsible body in administration. The opportunity should be presented by the person responsible for development.

In most cases it will be possible to gain a response or commitment at the time of the visit. In any event a time frame not to exceed ten days should be established for a response.

The payment schedule is subject to negotiation. It must not be superimposed upon the donor by the institution. Counselors should be prepared to negotiate payment over a period as long as five years. Many prospective donors will have made financial commitments for philanthropic giving as much as three years in advance. A financial commitment from a prospective donor in a four- or five-year time frame can be programmed to meet the need of the local church or institution. In each event, of course, the response must be firm, in writing, and state specifically the time of payment. In that event loans can be arranged against the deferred payment usually with little difficulty. Seldom is there attrition from the commitments of major donors.

Whether one is dealing with potential donors of a major or minor dimension three things need to be remembered: 1. the counselor must be fully informed and trained to present the overture; 2. the counselor must have a specific challenge to present to the prospective donor; and 3. the counselor must be in a peer situation with the prospective donor either in terms of vocation, economic station, or position in the structure of the community in terms of funding or life-style.

6

Selecting Members for the Stewardship Enlistment and Commitment Task Force

When one considers the fact that no counselor is to make more than four calls, and the number of individuals or families to be visited may range from forty to several thosand, this task force assumes an important responsibility. A task force of three persons certainly cannot do it all by themselves. An organizational procedure is essential.

First, enlistment. In the stewardship enlistment and commitment process it is suggested that captains be secured to enlist the services of ten counselors. If there are to be 100 counselors, the task force is responsible for enlisting the aid of ten captains and assisting them in their enlistment of ten counselors.

The three persons on the task force must be capable of challenging others. The captains they recruit should be capable and have strong personalities and the ability to recruit others. Water will not rise above its source; likewise the quality of the captains will not exceed the capability or the effectiveness of those responsible for the process.

Some captains will need guidance in and suggestions concerning the selection and enlistment of counselors, and it is important that the task force leaders are able to provide not only valid counsel but an introduction to potential counselors.

Those serving on the Stewardship Enlistment and Commitment Task Force must be capable not only of discerning and nurturing others but also have a broad acquaintanceship in the local church or organization in order that they may attain their objective quickly. While all members of the task force need not share the same skills, one or two of them must provide the key to enlistment, or recruitment, by knowing a large number of people and having the ability to pick out those who have leadership capability, are responsible, and can be depended upon to follow through with recruitment and training.

There is a general prejudice that the membership of such a task force must be mature in years and male. This is not so. Often those who have the broadest acquaintanceship and are capable of discerning leadership qualities, and assessing responsible service will be young and many times female. Even with today's emphasis on equal rights, those selecting task force members must face the fact that some capable leaders will not rally to the challenge and support of female enlisters. Therefore it will be well for the task force to consist of both men and women and they, as leaders, assess where they may be most effective in the leadership process. Sex, however, is not the only criteria. Personality, appearance, vocation, and education are equally important. Some prospective captains will not accept an invitation to serve because the person enlisting their services just does not please them personally, does not have the authority or enthusiasm to challenge them, or simply does not have an equal social position.

Potential captains do not need strong reasoning or valid appraisals to say no. Any reason will suffice if they are not interested in serving. However, it is important that no one decline the invitation before the overture is presented them for their personal service. A personal visit will be required in most cases.

Once the members of the task force are selected and trained, they are ready to seek commitments, obtaining the resources to fund ministry and mission as well as any capital funding needs. Securing a commitment entails three steps.

First, the presentation of the opportunity. Each captain and counselor must have an understanding of the institution, its needs, and current obligations. These must not be left to speculation. Each captain and counselor must be able to present the matter intelligently, enthusiastically, and effectively.

Second, the fielding of questions and especially changing a negative attitude to a positive orientation. Elements of negativism emerge most readily in persons when confronted by a financial challenge or need. The tendency to preserve financial resources rises strongly against competing elements for the same funding. The response of a counselor to a negative attitude should never be apologetic or supportive of the negative attitude. Any concurrence will result in an inadequate financial commitment by a donor. Negative attitudes must be countered with affirmative elements in a positive program environment.

Third, a consummation of the financial commitment. In most cases it is expedient that the donor's decision be made at the time the overture is presented and the response entered on the commitment form. Time does not bode well for average and modest contributors. It is different with major potential donors; often they need time to consult with their legal and financial counsel. In these events subsequent visits should be arranged to keep the process on schedule and to secure the commitment in adequate time. For these kinds of calls it is essential that the counselors be knowledgeable of the philanthropic opportunities our society provides and the time frame in which an affirmative response may be acceptable to the process. Special training provided counselors should include an up-date on tax provisions that will be important to consideration of support to the nonprofit venture.

One other urgent point confronts the Enlistment and Commitment Task Force. This is establishing and maintaining a schedule of the due dates for progress reports from captains and counselors, counselors reporting to captains, and captains reporting to the task force. This schedule should be followed religiously. The final report deadline must be clear in the minds of all who are sharing in the effort. Any delay beyond the deadline suggests that the effort has not been successful and always results in a lack of a sense of achievement until all reports are in and every financial commitment tabulated in the total.

When the Stewardship Enlistment and Commitment Task Force has nurtured the commitment process to a successful conclusion, it is important to recognize each captain and counselor with an award, certificate, or symbol for meritorious service. Never neglect to express the organization's gratitude for any service and time expended in the process.

The key to the total development process will lie with the persons recruited to serve on the Stewardship Enlistment and Commitment Task Force.

7

The Special Gifts Task Force

Few task forces can be of as great interest and effectiveness as the Special Gifts Task Force. My experience shows that persons are more eager to give when they know exactly how their money will be spent. While it may be difficult to interest regular contributors of modest means to increase their support by a dollar a month, it is not difficult to get them to buy a can of paint. While it may be difficult to interest regular contributors of average means to increase their support by five dollars a month, it is not difficult to get them to fund the sealing of a parking space in an organization's parking lot. While it may be difficult to interest substantial donors to increase their giving by perhaps 100 percent, it is not difficult to get them to fund an item of capital improvement or a major funding need as long as it is not in the budget.

The Special Gifts Task Force should put together a list of thirty-five designated gift opportunities for those interested in funding a special gift. The list should be available at all times. As items are funded from the list, other items should be listed to replace them. Before the list is made available to a potential donor, however, it—and any additions—should be approved by the administrative board of the organization.

In compiling such a list, the Special Gifts Task Force should first look at the organization's operational budget. In the area of operations the average organization faces its greatest squeeze; while special gifts are always welcome, they are useful to an organization only when they have an effect on the budget.

In a local church, a family may fund the floral arrangements for a Sunday's services, and although this is a nice gesture, it does not help with the organization's operational budget. If a donor would fund an issue of the Sunday bulletin, or program, the special gift would help the institution meet its budgetary goals. Perhaps as many as one-fifth of the items on the special gifts list may be lifted from the annual budget to help the organization underwrite the annual obligations.

The list should also include items not found in the annual budget. In many cases they are items important to the organization meeting its objective but not strong enough in priority to compete with expenses essential to the institution's survival. These may be items of capital, equipment, facilities, materials, or supplies. In many cases it will not be a single item but a group of items or a number of items.

A lounge may need refurbishing. This is a special gift opportunity that may be funded by one person or many. If the project is undertaken in concert with others, it would be possible for one person to fund the carpeting, another a lamp, another an occasional chair, another a couch, and still another a piano. Dozens of people could actually share in the project and sense the importance of their contribution.

Donors may share, as well, in funding one item of a set. Twenty-five gallons of paint may be needed to decorate a room or hall. Individual donors can pay for a can of paint. Forty folding chairs may be required for an assembly room. Donors may fund a single chair.

A challenge gift falls in the area of a unique special gift opportunity. I recall some years ago when the Central Presbyterian Church in Denver, Colorado was in need of an elevator; the parish was a facility several stories high and had many members of advanced years. In a visit with the senior pastor, the Reverend Dr. James Emerson, my father presented the challenge that he would contribute the first two thousand dollars for an elevator if the pastor could raise the rest of the money. Of course the objective was met in a rather short period of time.

The Special Gifts Task Force could well envision other significant gifts that may include buildings and grounds, programs and services, equipment and supplies.

Buildings and grounds could include a chapel, education wing, or recreation center; grounds for parking, a playground, or a memorial garden for those who will be cremated and want a sacred place for the respose of their ashes.

Programs and services could include a trust fund to finance a series of lectures, a concert, or a staff person for a particular ministry or service to a parish or area.

Equipment and supplies could include a riding mower for the organization's lawn care, audiovisual equipment for organizational services, or a video cassette for a particular age group.

How will these needs, or opportunities, become known to prospective donors? First, once the list is completed, it should be placed in the hands of every staff person and officer to share with prospective contributors. When first introducing the opportunity, the entire list may be included in a special mailing.

Second, it is recommended that three items be listed in at least one issue of a newsletter each month going to members and friends. One item should be modest in cost or a project in which a number of donors may share. A second item should be of intermediate size, ranging in cost from five hundred to a thousand dollars. A third should be a large and significant challenge type. If the three special gift opportunities do not draw any support, they should not be published month after month. Unless a matter is of great emergency, it should not be listed more frequently than three times in a single year.

Third, with significant items the task force should endeavor to pair a need with a potential donor and present a personal overture to that donor. The Profiles Task Force can provide the Special Gifts Task Force with the names and background material of those who would most likely be interested in funding a particular need.

In order that every special gift provide strength to the organization I strongly urge that a 15 percent surcharge be placed on those items not included in the operational budget to cover administrative expenses. This is both legitimate and proper, for no special gift may be gained by an institution without costs being incurred by the organization. No donor should expect the organization to assume this cost.

As items are funded, it is essential that the fact be publicized. When possible, the name of the donor should be listed with the gift as a means of providing incentive for others to fund more special gift opportunities. Certainly some will prefer to remain anonymous. The announcement of an anonymous gift will still help to stimulate additional gifts and funding. The process has a domino effect, and the funding of special gifts fall in line rather rapidly as the opportunities become known to potential donors.

Many special gift ideas will emerge from potential donors, rather than from the organization and its officers or leadership. Therefore, it is expedient that the names, addresses, and telephone numbers of the Special Gifts Task Force be published from time to time in order that prospective donors with special interest may contact a responsible person who can assist them in making a special gift.

8

Selecting Members for the Special Gifts Task Force

In recruiting leaders for the Special Gifts Task Force three things should be kept in mind.

First, it is important that the special gift opportunities actually increase the capability of the organization in attaining its objectives and equip it with the means to serve its people more effectively.

Some special gifts offered to organizations should not be accepted if they are not appropriate to either the organization's need or purpose. In this event, the task force should ask the prospective donor to consider a more appropriate designation. However, if the prospective donor is not open to alternatives and the gift would be a burden, rather than a blessing to the oganization, there should be no hesitancy in saying "no" or suggesting that the gift be given to another organization that could utilize the opportunity more advantageously.

The members of the Special Gifts Task Force must be in the life, work, and programs of the organization; aware of the needs of the organization for administration and service; and determined that the special gifts received will be commensurate with the organization's needs in terms of quality, quantity, and importance.

Second, it is important that regular dialogue is sustained between the Special Gifts Task Force and the leadership of the institution. The Special Gifts Task Force should always be up-to-date on any equipment, facilities, and materials needed.

Third, it is expedient that the members of the Special Gifts Task

Force have a broad association among the organization's potential donors and that they be respected as honorable and reliable persons. The trust placed by potential donors in an organization will be no greater than that directed toward those providing leadership in this process.

Hearing of a potential donor's interest, it will be important for the Special Gifts Task Force to arrange for a meeting to discuss the special gift opportunity with the potential donor. In general, larger gifts are the result of personal contact by a member of the Special Gifts Task Force or another knowledgeable person.

In the light of these needs, the following guidelines may prove valid in the recruitment process.

One person serving on the Special Gifts Task Force may be a person who has been a leader over the years in the organization's life and work. This person would know the organizational leadership, as well as the organization's needs, and project the image of a knowledgeable person in the organization's life and work.

A second person serving on the Special Gifts Task Force may be a person who has a broad reputation among the members and friends of the organization, as well as across the community. This person may be in public life, an educator, or a community worker, a person to whom potential donors may easily relate. This person should not only be well known but have a pleasing personality and should be one who may be approached quite easily even by a stranger.

A third person serving on the Special Gifts Task Force may well be a person who serves as a purchasing agent, a buyer, a manufacturer's representative, or a person whose occupation relates to quality control. This person is in a position to know quality merchandise, a fair price, and the appropriateness of gifts. So often special gifts are provided whose standards simply do not meet the institutional need. Many donors will consider equipment needs from the standpoint of domestic usage, rather than institutional and organizational usage, and the quality of the gift is such that it does not adequately meet the long-term needs of the organization.

These three types represented on the Special Gifts Task Force will be most helpful to the special gifts opportunity by sustaining rapport with leadership, popularity among prospective potential donors, and quality standards for those things brought to the organization's life and work through designated funding.

9

The Memorials Task Force

No donation provides as great an opportunity to seal the relationship between the organization and the donor as memorial gifts. A relationship between an individual and an institution based on a tribute to a loved one not only results in substantial and meaningful gifts but lays the foundation for significant giving of a current and deferred nature. Regular budget support and sometimes bequests will come from those who have shared in the memorial opportunity.

One simple procedure the task force can introduce is the opportunity for an individual to present a gift to a memorial fund as an expression of sympathy to families and relatives and recognition of a person who has died. Gifts to a memorial fund may range in size from very modest sums to significantly large gifts representing hundreds of thousands of dollars.

Five elements are essential for the program to work effectively.

First, the recognition of the person whose memory is honored as a result of the gift. A Book of Remembrance is recommended for the permanent record. It includes the name of the person remembered and the name of the individual, or individuals, who have contributed funding to perpetuate the witness of the deceased person. This book should be attractively bound, inscribed in an artistic fashion, and displayed in a case where it will be preserved and safeguarded.

Second, an announcement of each memorial gift to the survivors of the deceased person commemorated. The announcement should be attractively engraved and artistically lettered to announce that a contribution has been made to the memorial fund in memory of a loved one. The amount of the gift should not be inscribed in the Book of Remembrance or included in the engraved announcement sent to the family. These sums should be kept in confidence. However, it would not be inappropriate for a family member to be told the sources and the amounts of gifts in those cases where the information is available and unrestricted.

Third, acknowledgment to the donor. An acknowledgment similar in form to the announcement above should be prepared for the donor. It should include the name of the person making the contribution, the name of the person whose memory is being honored through the gift, and the amount of the contribution to the organization. It would be appropriate, as well, to indicate the way in which the name of the person honored, as well as the name of the donor, will be perpetuated (in a Book of Remembrance or some such thing).

Fourth, periodical publication of the persons whose memories are honored through contributions, as well as the names of the donors. This will not only enhance the importance of the gifts and the process but call attention to an opportunity in which others may share.

Fifth, publication of the expenditure of undesignated gifts. Undesignated gifts may provide for the funding of capital improvements, equipment, special projects or programs. It is appropriate when such funds are used that the fact be published announcing the project or program to which the funding has gone and those persons whose remembrance has been enhanced by the gifts. This, too, is a means of promoting the memorial gift opportunity to prospective donors.

The Memorials Task Force must also provide opportunity for prospective donors to make designated gifts that will perpetuate the memory of those they choose to honor. As in the case of the Special Gifts Task Force, a listing of approximately thirty-five items appropriate as memorial gifts should be available for prospective donors.

There are three considerations in selecting items for the listing of donor opportunities.

First, the item should be significant enough to constitute a special gift as a tribute to an individual or individuals. A can of paint for decorating a room would not qualify but the cost of painting a mural might. The contribution for funding a single chair in a classroom would not quality, but buying a pew in a sanctuary or chapel would be appropriate. The sealing, or paving, of a parking space would not qualify, but funding for landscaping an area may well constitute a memorial gift.

Second, the purpose of the organization should be extended and the program enhanced as a result of the memorial contribution. In no event should the gift be incongruous to the interests, concerns, or priorities of the individual, or individuals, honored or the organization.

The local church or organization will gain greatly in potential for perpetuity as an institution through the receiving of memorials and special gifts in remembrance of persons who have died.

10

Selecting Members for
the Memorials Task Force

Inasmuch as Christianity holds sacred the "communion of the saints" special consideration should be given the qualifications of those person sitting on the Memorials Task Force.

In selecting the chairperson I would seek a person possessing those qualities one would expect to find in a funeral director. This person should be patient, sympathetic, and attentive to a donor's interests, concerns, and dedication in establishing a memorial for a departed family member or friend. Since many persons interested in this type of philanthropic opportunity are advanced in years, it is appropriate that the chairperson of the task force be a mature individual in both age and experience.

Whether or not the chairperson of the Memorials Task Force is a woman, it is essential that one or more women serve on the task force, and at least one of them should be of mature age. The vast majority of persons making memorial gifts are mature women. Often they will look to another woman from in their peer group for assistance in this area. While the woman may not be qualified to consummate the arrangement with the potential donor, she will be able to assist the process in a constructive manner, and both the size and quality of the gift may increase as a result of her involvement.

The emphasis so far has been on selecting persons for the task force who have attained seniority; yet it is expedient that a person representing the young and middle-aged group be included as well. There are two reasons: First, a primary purpose of a memorial gift is to extend the identification and witness of the person, or persons, into the future. The persons on the task force representing young or middle-aged persons are indeed representing those persons who may well benefit the most from the gift given in memorium. Second, there are young and middle-aged persons who want to honor parents, spouses, children, and others through a memorial gift. Their interests may often best be understood by someone in their age group. The soliciting of memorials need not be confined to the Memorials Task Force. Others may be recruited in special cases.

In presenting memorial opportunities the task force may face three questions:

Who is the potential donor?
What is the nature of the memorial gift, or gift of remembrance?
Who can best present the opportunity to the potential donor?

It is erroneous to assume that it does not matter who presents the memorial opportunity. It does. The person presenting the opportunity must be one whom the prospective donor will welcome, appreciating their concern and interest.

It would be inappropriate to conclude this chapter without giving some guidelines for identifying prospective donors and establishing the means by which their doors may be opened to the task force to discuss memorial gift giving.

A general mailing to the constituency introducing the opportunity of memorial gifts and those persons serving on the task force is a proper beginning. From time to time, in the regular publications of the local church or organization, it is appropriate to list memorial gift opportunities and to ask that any person who may be interested in these, or other memorial opportunities, contact a member of the task force.

The best way of developing interest in memorial gift opportunities is through the announcement and publication of gifts at the time they are presented. In this way others may announce their interest in the opportunity.

It would be most appropriate for the Memorials Task Force to orchestrate the dedication of memorial gifts in connection with the worship service on All Saints' Sunday. Gifts received over the preceding twelve months can be announced as well as printed in the dedication program. The act of consecration will provide the same recognition to all gifts, whether large or small, and the widow's mite will have as great significance in the process as the large gift that may not represent nearly as much dedication or sacrifice.

In a sense, the responsibilities of the Memorials Task Force extend beyond presenting overtures for gifts of remembrance. Rather, they include the total process of securing the gifts and incorporating them fully into the life and work of the institution as extensions of the lives and faith of individuals whose memories are honored.

11

The Gift Annuity Task Force

When serving as a consultant to St. Stephen's Episcopal Church in Sewickly, Pennsylvania, I was assigned by the parish for several days to meet with interested individuals to discuss various philanthropic opportunities that might be appropriate for their particular situation. One of the individuals was an eighty-three-year-old woman who began the conversation by saying, "I'm sick! I've been a member of St. Stephen's Church for more than sixty years. There has never been a program in which I have not shared. Now my accountant tells me that I can make no further contributions to my church except for regular budget support. What can I do?"

We discussed her situation at length and discovered that she had a reasonable annual income from her investment portfolio, no other persons dependent upon her, and only a niece to benefit from her estate. I spoke to her concerning the gift annuity opportunity. Simply stated, by making a contribution to St. Stephen's Church in exchange for a gift annuity she would receive a return of 10.6 percent of which only 29.6 percent would be taxable income.

For each one thousand dollars contributed as a gift annuity, $373.96 would qualify as a charitable contribution in the year that it was given, with a carry-over of five succeeding years should charitable contributions exceed the statute limit.

If the donor were to present appreciated securities in payment of the gift annuity, the tax on capital gains would be computed on the actuarial value, rather than the market value of the securities, in the agreement. In this event the actuarial value was $626.04.

This elderly woman became interested in a gift annuity and enthused about sharing in the capital funding program in this manner. In discovering the benefits of the gift annuity, the woman's accountant arranged for securities in the amount of ten thousand dollars to be transferred to St. Stephen's Church to fund the gift annuity. She more than doubled her annual income and in addition avoided all federal taxation on capital gain because the actuarial value exceeded the cost of the original securities.

There are many persons in each local church who are anxious to support both current and capital needs, but their financial position limits participation. Income must be sustained from whatever investments they have. The gift annuity provides an economically feasible, opportunity for many persons in this category.

The following things need to be emphasized:

The gift annuity is not an investment opportunity but a philanthropic instrument for supporting charitable organizations. One must not compare income or investment opportunities with either the rate of return or the tax factors resulting from a gift annuity. Benefits may be greater, or lesser, in one or the other. The gift annuity provides an opportunity for an individual to make a charitable contribution without depriving themselves of an annual income. The rates and tax factors are established by the National Committee on Gift Annuities in cooperation with the U.S. Treasury Department. Rates are established at three year intervals and are effective with new agreements.

Funds contributed in exchange for a gift annuity constitute an irrevocable contribution by the donor. It is as though the money was placed in a collection plate or mailed as a charitable contribution. The donor has no claim on the organization other than those in the agreement. The organization has no obligation to the donor other than those incorporated in the terms of the agreement. The sums contributed for a gift annuity are lost to both the donor and the estate.

The gift annuity should not be considered a substitute for a charitable bequest in a last will and testament. The gift annuity provides opportunity for the donor to make a contribution while he or she is alive and can enjoy the benefits that may result from expanding programs or securing capital improvements. The gift annuity is an instrument for a current funding opportunity.

The gift annuity may be established by any donor at any age. Minimum contributions are usually in the amount of one thousand dollars. Annual income increases with the age of the annuitant at the time the agreement is written, and the older the annuitant, the greater the benefit in terms of annual income. tax exclusion on annual income, and gift value as a charitable contribution at the time the gift is given and the contract written. Those sixty years of age and older will probably have the greatest interest in the gift annuity opportunity.

The gift annuity may be issued to a donor providing income for two persons or the survivor. These may, or may not, be related. In this event the income and tax factors will not be as great as in the case of a single-life agreement, but income continues for as long as one of the two persons live. The two-life gift annuity is usually the better instrument for elderly couples.

A second instrument for philanthropic giving is the deferred-payment gift annuity. It is similar to the gift annuity with the exception that the donor specifies the time that annual income will be paid to the person, or persons, benefiting from the agreement. For example, a person forty years of age may share in the deferred-payment gift annuity opportunity and determine that income is to begin at age sixty-two, sixty-five, or some other time. The income can be quite substantial and the tax factors quite attractive to potential donors.

The deferred-payment gift annuity perhaps has its greatest appeal to self-employed persons who are placing maximum investments in individual retirement accounts and tax shelters but are still concerned with retirement income as well as philanthropic giving. The deferred-payment gift annuity falls under the Internal Revenue Code as charitable contributions and is not limited in any way by the terms applicable to individual retirement plans.

The gift annuity and the deferred-payment gift annuity should be included in the charitable contribution opportunities provided by each local church and voluntary group. Several steps can be taken to present the gift annuity and the deferred-payment gift annuity opportunities.

First, a descriptive brochure or flier should be prepared for distribution to the constituency and available to prospective donors at any time. The brochure should include a response form addressed to the Gift Annuity Task Force on which a prospective donor may list the age(s) of the annuitant(s) and request an IRS computation to gain the full particulars related to annual income and taxes. Those seeking this information should know that the process is confidential and the prospective donor is under no obligation to consider the opportunity any further.

Second, periodically the line *Inquire into our gift annuity program* or *Have you considered a gift annuity?* should be included in your publications on a regular basis, at least once a month. In addition articles illustrating the benefits of both the gift annuity and the deferred-payment gift annuity should be published quarterly.

Third, an excellent way to promote the gift annuity opportunity is by publishing names of donors at the time agreements are written. If the donor requests anonymity, the organization should announce from time to time that a certain number of gift annuity agreements have been made over the past thirty, sixty, or ninety days. Securing the first agreement is usually the most difficult. Once the opportunity is known as an actual instrument utilized by members and friends, others will respond.

Fourth, the presentation of a plaque or certificate suitable for framing to the donor in recognition of participation in the gift annuity program will prove helpful. Most donors will be proud to display it at their place of business or residence, and it will stimulate interest in others to respond in a similar manner.

Fifth, an honor roll of gift annuitants should be published in annual reports of the organization. If donors prefer, they may be identified anonymously. Many will allow publication of their name, and this will motivate other donors to consider the opportunity—especially among peer groups. In no case should the listing include the amounts contributed by or the benefits provided to any annuitant or donor.

The policies of the organization relating to both the gift annuity and the deferred-payment gift annuity will determine the opportunities that potential donors will have in funding the organization.

If the organization has a large volume in gift annuities, it may well self-insure all annuities. In this event no donor will have the opportunity to fund a current need through a gift annuity. The resources will not be available to meet the funding needs of the local church or agency until the demise of the annuitant, or the survivor in the case of the two-life agreements.

If the organization does not self-insure, and each agreement is insured by a qualified company to assure the annual income to each annuitant, the funding beyond the insuring costs is available to meet immediate funding needs in the organization. For organizations with limited participation in the gift annuity this is the recommended route to follow.

Those organizations or local churches having large volume in gift annuities should provide both options: self-insuring to meet deferred needs in program or endowment and insured annuity income to meet current needs.

If insuring an individual agreement, the organization will be required to expend approximately 50 percent of the funds contributed as a gift annuity for the insuring process.

The Gift Annuity Task Force has the responsibility of explaining the process to the prospective donor and matching the donor with the opportunity that will best serve their interests.

The gift annuity is probably the least used instrument for philanthropic giving in eleemosynary organizations today, and it is the instrument that provides the greatest opportunity for expanding donor support to local churches and nonprofit organizations in the current period.

12

Selecting Members for the Gift Annuity Task Force

As those responsible for recruiting individuals for the various task forces come to the task of selecting possible recruits for the Gift Annuity Task Force, they invariably turn to persons who work in the insurance field either as administrators or agents. I suppose this is logical as it is recommended that some organizations, and perhaps all, insure annuities. In the larger organizations, those agreements that provide resources for current funding need to be insured. In the smaller organizations, all agreements are insured to guarantee the financial credibility of the process and the annuitants' annual income. The process obviously moves in the direction of the insurance industry.

However, one will soon discover that those serving as administrators or agents in the insurance industry have difficulty understanding the annuity as a philanthropic instrumentality. The annuity issued by an insurance company is a tool to assure income on a regular basis. The gift annuity is a means of making a charitable contribution without depriving the donor of an annual income. The primary purpose of the first is to benefit the investor and the primary purpose of the second is to benefit the charitable organization. The Gift Annuity Task Force is not an insurance sales force. In the light of their experience, few in the industry will serve a task force well.

Where, then, does one begin?

The first person I would select would be a retired person with strong philanthropic leanings, dedicated to the objectives of the organization, and comfortable in sharing the instrumentality of the gift annuity as an educational opportunity. Retired persons from the field of education, either administrators or teachers, provide excellent service in this area for a number of reasons.

First, they are educators and not salespersons. They can bring their experience to bear on informing individuals and helping them to understand the benefits available through the gift annuity opportunity. These persons will be less apt to use a hard sell, to force a person to do other than what they really want to do in connection with the gift annuity opportunity. This is important.

Second, educators are well respected. While teaching no longer has the respect it had fifty years ago as a profession, there are few professions in which persons generally have as great a confidence and respect for personal opinion. Although educators have always had a modest income, they have generally been good managers of their financial resources, and this reputation is a valuable asset to the gift annuity presentation.

Third, those in the field of education can field questions well. Questions answered directly and honestly will reassure people and influence their decision about the Gift Annuity.

The second person I would select for the Gift Annuity Task Force would be a woman who has experience in the business world, a woman who has held an executive or managerial position and is considered successful. Age is not a factor.

The third person to serve on the Gift Annuity Task Force may be a person who is known and recognized for philanthropic interests and services. This person may be self-employed and familiar with the tax shelters and benefits relevant to both the gift annuity and the deferred-payment gift annuity. Philanthropic interests and services must be evident; the person must be one who is generous with his or her financial resources and active, as well as interested, in the nonprofit sector. While these interests must have some connection to the organization for which the gift annuity is secured, the activities and interests need not be confined to the particular organization. The person may be known best of all for his or her interest in a hospital, YMCA, YWCA, or community service group. A person dedicted to humanitarian and voluntary organizations, as well as voluntary giving, will be a great asset to the task force.

The guidelines provided for these three task-force members are broad enough that any local church or organization will be able to enlist and equip persons to serve the gift annuity opportunity well.

Remember, the areas of importance are not salesmanship or investment. The task is to assist prospective donors in philanthropic giving while sustaining financial income to ensure financial capability to meet life's daily needs.

13

The Wills and Bequests Task Force

There is a general assumption that a person does not need a will. Inasmuch as the vast majority of persons in the United States do not have a will, the assumption is valid. As a result, each state has, through legislative process, established the terms whereby the estates of individuals are administered and distributed upon their death. States also provide opportunity for individuals to exercise their personal rights in the distribution of their possessions according to their best judgment through the preparation of a will. In reviewing the statutes, most would reinforce one's personal decision in the distribution of their assets. As a result, all persons truly do not need a will but if one is to exercise personal privileges and rights relating to the administration and distribution of one's material remains, a person must have a will.

There is another assumption that wills are instruments only for the aged or persons near death. If a person waits until old age when physical faculties may be failing to write a will, it may be contested on the grounds that the individual was not mentally alert or physically able to make proper and responsible decisions.

Although every person has a will through state statute, every person should take full advantage of the opportunity to exercise stewardship over all of his or her material resources for as long as the administration and distribution of resources are subject to an individual's decision making. Remember, we are responsible stewards not only as long as life lasts but as long as our decisions determine the use of our resources.

We seldom consider the fact that when parents take out a life insurance policy on their child they select to name one or more beneficiaries, and this becomes a "bequest" in a child's estate. When an application is made for a baby's or child's Social Security number, the designation of a guardian is required in each event, and at that moment there is the dictation of a bequest. For most persons, this is the extent of their personal estate planning, and no other consideration or designations are made until the minor becomes independent, dependent upon someone else, or marries.

Because every person, even every child, has a will, the Wills and Bequests Task Force becomes an important part of Christian stewardship. The Wills and Bequests Task Force not only assumes responsibility for encouraging every individual to have a will, but in the Christian community it is especially important that the will be a testament of faith.

Individuals have a responsibility to those persons who depend upon them (a spouse, a dependent child, a relative, etc.) Their wills must provide for dependents as adequately as resources will allow. Similarly, individuals have responsibilities to the household of faith in which they hold membership, and the concerns of the church's mission should be equally important to individuals in the expression of their faith.

There are two reasons why the religious experience should be included in a will: 1. the Last Will and Testament should be an expression of one's faith, those things most earnestly believed by the individual, and 2. the Last Will and Testament should strengthen the ministry and mission for which resources are designated just as they have during the life time of the individual donor.

The Wills and Bequests Task Force then must assume their role understanding that their task is to impress upon the individual the importance of personal estate planning, the significance of the Last Will and Testament in that plan, and the value of designated bequests as an extended witness to faith and an extension of life through work that will be strengthed by persons' material resources.

How can this be accomplished? Since so great a number of persons must be reached, an important function of the Wills and Bequests Task Force will lie in the interpretation and information process based on the idea that "an informed people will do the right thing." Information must be given to members and friends in the local church or organization on a regular basis. The following procedures will prove helpful.

First, inlcude brief paragraphs in the regular Sunday bulletin, or organ, distributed to parishoners on a frequent basis. These paragraphs may deal with the following:

The importance of personal estate planning
The importance of each person having a will
Opportunities for general and designated bequests
Listings of persons who have made a bequest to the organization
Listings of opportunities for funding ministry and mission through designated bequests

These brief paragraphs and listings will be among the most important pieces of communication instituted by the Wills and Bequests Task Force.

Second, include articles in the regular newsletter of the organization. The themes listed above will be appropriate for the newsletter articles as well. While the articles will not be read word for word to the extent that the paragraphs will, they will be more descriptive in nature. Those having a special interest in a particular item will gain considerable information. In most cases the task force, or individual members of the task force, may not know of this interest or need for information.

The paragraphs should not exceed five sentences and the articles should not exceed five paragraphs in length.

Third, there are numerous fliers, folders, and brochures available for mass distribution either without charge or at modest cost that may be obtained for both special mailings or included as inserts. Recognize the fact that items of this type will receive greater attention in special mailings than if they are included as an insert in a bulletin or newsletter. An exception, of course, would be if the bulletin or newsletter highlighted one of the topics in an issue and the insert complemented the subject matter.

Paragraphs should appear bimonthly, articles quarterly, and special mailings or inserts semiannually. "Remember your church (organization) in your will" should be in each publication. The annual reports, directory, and other publications should include the forms for general and designated bequests.

There will often be a tendency for the Wills and Bequests Task

Force to look to denominational, banking, and insurance sources for fliers and brochures relating to personal estate planning. Although involving an expenditure of funds, fliers and brochures prepared uniquely for the particular local church or organization will be far more effective and more likely read and used by the reader.

Seminars, workshops, and panels should be scheduled through the course of the year geared to particular age groups and types of persons. These should include

single adults
young adults
single parents
adults approaching the retirement years
retired persons
widows and unmarried women,
widowers and bachelors
family groups with no emphasis upon any individual grouping

A panel for any group may consist of an attorney, trust officer at a banking institution, investment counselor, pastor, or denominational foundation representative. A good format to follow is a ten minute statement from each panelist on personal estate planning from his or her experience and point of view; fifteen minutes for the exchange of ideas between panel members; a refreshment period; and an additional forty-five minutes to one hour for persons to ask questions of any panel member.

On some occasions it will be appropriate to present films or slides. On still other occasions it will be well to have one person speak on a particular aspect of personal estate planning. Presentations, in terms of form or content, should not repeat a previous one. Numerous events, as well as numerous approaches, will be expedient and necessary if the major portion of the constituency is to be reached.

One fact must be kept uppermost in the task force's services: The exercise of Christian stewardship requires each person to have a will. Whether or not the church is included in one's will is actually secondary to the primary concern, namely, that individuals prove responsible of the trust placed in them by our Lord in the stewardship of material resources, family, and those for whom they bear a responsibility.

14

Selecting Members for the Wills and Bequests Task Force

While we are concerned in this book with the task of developing resources for ministry and mission, consideration of the Wills and Bequests Task Force makes me realize that the responsibility extends beyond merely developing funding for the local church and related organizations. It includes the development of responsible stewardship in the lives of individuals on an everyday level. Some persons need a will because of family responsibilities, professional interests, or social and organizational opportunities. Some persons need a will because others depend upon them and their good judgment in financial and administrative responsibilities. Many persons will desire that their will give expression to their faith in Christ and hope in the Gospel!

All of these concerns should also be of interest and important to the Wills and Bequests Task Force, and it is essential that appropriate personnel be recruited to meet these needs.

One person well qualified to serve on the Wills and Bequests Task Force is a person whose services, vocationally or avocationally, fall in the area of long-range planning. Usually these persons are able to see designs for the future beyond both their life span and their personal gain. Not only do they have their eye on the future, but they have their feet on the ground.

This type will be especially valuable to the Wills and Bequests Task Force because they will be able to keep in focus both the needs of the organization, as well as the interests of the prospective donor, as they look to the future even beyond their life span.

This type of person can gain the respect of those who are considering personal estate planning. In addition through their contacts, they will be able to recruit panelists or speakers to share their expertise on personal designs for the future.

A second person to be secured for membership on the Wills and Bequests Task Force is a counselor in either a school or social service agency. Much of the decision making that takes place in personal estate planning will depend upon an individual receiving guidance in understanding the implications of the decisions made as well as the importance of their decisions relative to both persons and values. In some cases individuals will seek out this task force member to enlist assistance in exploring possibilities, considering options, and determining the best course for the future as a result of objectively viewing their situation from a perspective beyond themselves.

The third person to be secured for service on the Wills and Bequests Task Force should be an educator. The presentation of panels, lectureships, and programs is an educational process, and few will be more capable of determining the design than a qualified educator. It is not necessary that the educator serving on the task force be professionally connected to a higher institution of learning or even a secondary public or private school. Persons in elementary education may qualify as well. The person who will serve best will be someone who understands the task of communicating to an individual's understanding.

Let me emphasize the importance of both sexes serving on the Wills and Bequests Task Force. Together the members should represent a full spectrum of life. All should not be the same age; all should not be senior citizens; all should not be affluent. Each should complement the others in terms of age and expertise.

The effectiveness of this task force will be learned in years to come, and those who serve on it will determine the results that the local church will gain from their contribution.

15

The Real Estate and Personal Property Task Force

One will seldom drive through an older, affluent section of a city or community without seeing a number of large facilities containing the offices and service centers for community organizations. The Council of Churches in Buffalo, New York; the Urban League in Springfield, Illinois; and United Ministries in Seattle, Washington provide good illustrations. Each residence was provided to the nonprofit organization as a charitable contribution either as an outright gift or a bequest from a deceased donor.

In more cases than not, a gift of real estate or personal property is unsolicited by the organization, and when it is the result of the donor's personal estate planning, the organization does not know of the donation until the time the will is probated. If eleemosynary organizations receive such capital gifts without solicitation, one can imagine the great potential available through philanthropic giving if persons are educated concerning the opportunities.

There are five types of capital gifts of real estate that living donors can make.

First, there is the opportunity to present a gift of residential property. In this event the donor has a sizable charitable contribution for tax purposes and does not pay taxes on the capital gains that may have resulted from the increasing value of the property during the donor's proprietorship. Often a prospective donor assumes that the only residential property of use to a nonprofit organization or a local church is property that may be used by the institution for the residence of a staff person, offices, or program facilities. Therefore, properties that are not contiguous, or near, the organization's facilities are deemed of little importance to many donors.

Residential property can provide capital resources to an organization, and the trustees can determine whether to keep the property in their investment portfolio for leasing to individuals or another organization or to sell the property and invest the proceeds another way. I advise converting such gifts to cash as soon as possible. Generally, investment in residential property yields a lower return than other kinds of investments.

Second, there is the opportunity to present a gift of residential property with right of estate. In this event the donors deed a property over to the institution with the understanding that they are to have the privilege of occupying the facility for as long as they live or as long as they desire the use of it. The institution is required to keep the property until vacated by the donor unless other conditions are made when conveying the title to the organization.

The charitable contribution value is available to the donor at the time the deed is transferred, and tax advantages fully computed at that time.

Separate agreements may be made concerning the obligations to be assumed by the organization and the donor relative to repair, maintenance, taxes, and insurance. The more expenses the donor assumes, the greater the value of the gift for tax purposes.

Third, there is the opportunity to present a gift of commercial property. The property may have served its purpose as far as the donor is concerned and have limited resale value. The local church or nonprofit organization can often convert such properties to extend their community service, provide the facilities for another agency, or raze the existing building to make the land available for other usage.

In the event the organization does not need the facility, it may prefer to receive the title subject to sale. In that event the liability, care, and insuring of the property remain with the donor until a buyer can be found.

Some commerical property presented to an organization will be nothing other than undeveloped land.

Fourth, there is the opportunity to present farmland. Usually this type opportunity will be welcomed by a potential donor in connection with a gift annuity or in establishing a charitable remainder trust or unitrust. In some cases the donor may elect to deed only a portion of a farm to the nonprofit organization.

In this event the organization must determine whether they will retain the title, arrange for operational services through the sharing of costs and profits, or maintain the facility in their investment portfolio. The organization may choose to receive the title to the farm, or farmland, subject to sale. The same conditioins would apply as in the case of a gift of commercial property.

Fifth, there is the opportunity of presenting oil or mineral rights. In most cases when such gifts are offered the drilling for oil or the mining of minerals is in production, and the asset is removed from the donor's portfolio to accommodate charitable contribution advantages for tax purposes.

As in the case of real estate, personal property falls into several categories as well.

First, there is the gift of personal property that is strictly personal in terms of clothing and household furnishings. Hardly a local church is not experienced in rummage and next-to-new sales.

Many local churches or organizations will dispose of all personal property of a deceased person for the heirs as a service to them. The local church naturally receives the proceeds from this portion of the estate, and the estate is provided receipts to qualify as charitable contributions to the organization.

Second, there are gifts of works of art. These may, or may not, be retained by the organization. In many cases, the local church will have no use for them at all. However, gifts or art provide an attractive philanthropic opportunity to the donor, for they are free from tax assessments on capital gains during the time the object was owned by the donor. The local church or agency may recieve art as outright gifts or subject to sale as they choose.

Third, there are gifts of equipment that are of a personal nature. These may consist of office furniture, copy machines, computer equipment, and the hundred and one things that go into personal and corporate living in the twentieth century.

Fourth, there are gifts of securities and life insurance policies. Most persons experienced in the investment field will choose to present appreciated securities to the local church or agency in paying their financial commitment. Those having less need of life insurance because of fewer dependents or obligations will prefer to transfer the ownership of a policy for insurance to a local church or agency, and at the same time name the organization the irrevocable beneficiary under the policy.

In outlining the potential for gifts of real estate and personal property the functions of the task force handling those gifts readily fall in line. Their primary task is to make known the opportunities and the interest of the organization in assisting prospective donors in their personal estate planning. Numerous procedures will be required.

First, the preparation and distribution of an appropriate handout to describe the various opportunities available to prospective donors. It should be distributed to the mailing list of the local church initially, available in the literature rack, and mailed to select prospective donors at appropriate times.

Second, the brief identification of donor opportunities in church or agency publications. The Information and Interpretation Task Force should include announcements in the weekly bulletin and monthly newsletter on real estate or personal property gifts.

Third, seminars on gifts of real estate and personal property to select groups from time to time.

Fourth, the announcement of gifts when received. Initially one will discover certain members providing their annual support through appreciated securities. The purpose need not be known to the membership and constituency, but if the announcement is made that a number of shares of a particular stock has been given by a member or friend, it will stimulate interest in other prospective donors who simply have not thought of such a gift.

One will discover, after implementing the emphasis on real estate and personal property gifts by the Real Estate and Personal Property Task Force, that it will have a domino effect in the organization. From time to time significant gifts will be received that simply would not have come had it not been for elevating an understanding of the process and the interest of the local church to assist their members and friends in the utilization of these types of opportunities.

16

Selecting Members for the Real Estate and Personal Property Task Force

When considering the types of persons to be selected for the Real Estate and Personal Property Task Force, the following conditions may well be kept in mind.

One or more persons serving on the Real Estate and Personal Property Task Force should own property. They need not own more than their private residence, and even that need not be unencumbered, but they should be known in the parish and community as property holders. A person holding both residential and commercial property will lend greater credibility to the task force as seen by prospective donors; but the person need not be, and likely should not be, a real estate broker. Such a person serving on the task force could present a conflict of interest, and this would be detrimental to both the individual and the organization.

A second person serving on the task force may well be vocationally, or avocationally, related to the fine arts—through education, community involvement, or known interests. Since the local church is not deeply involved in the fine arts as far as painting and sculpturing are concerned, it is essential that an individual well versed and gifted in these areas hold membership on the task force to be available to confer with a prospective donor about such an interest.

In regard to the two types just recommended, I am not suggesting that they be capable of appraising the value of a gift off the cuff or providing ready answers to prospective donors concerning the need for a gift by the local church or organization. In almost every case they will be the instrument through which experts are brought in to assist both the donor and the organization in processing the gift.

In considering the effectiveness of task forces I have urged limiting the number of members to three persons. While some task forces certainly will enlist the aid of others on an occasional, or full-time, basis, it is best when decision-making processes are limited to no more than three persons.

It is expedient that an educator be the third member of the task force. Because the opportunities for philanthropic giving are so broad and making the right decision so crucial to prospective donors (especially those presenting large gifts) that kind of background is essential for someone to educate prospective donors in both the opportunity and the process.

Although unessential, it is expedient that membership on the task force represent both sexes and persons selected from the age of forty-five years and over. Younger persons may well relate to the fine arts in a most capable and unique way. However, those who usually make contributions of art will have reached middle age and tend to have more confidence in those from their peer age.

In the course of their service it is essential that the members of the Real Estate and Personal Property Task Force become well informed concerning taxes as they relate to the gifts of real estate and personal property and the philanthropic instruments that may be best utilized in serving the donor's current, and long-term, interest.

Service on the task force may require a great deal of time. No one should be enlisted who is unwilling to serve or does not understand that this will become a position of reasonably high priority in serving the local church or organization.

17

The Charitable Remainder Trust Task Force

In proceeding through the chapters of this book, one will note that I have tended to move from the simplest of procedures for philanthropic giving to those that are more complex, from philanthropies that will be utilized almost universally to those that will be taken advantage of by a few either because of age or affluence. In a sense we come to the peak of the monolith of philanthropic processes as we consider the Charitable Remainder Trust.

By and large the persons interested in the charitable remainder trust are those who are philanthropically inclined, interested in regular income, and determined to reduce their responsibilities in handling their investment portfolio. At the same time they are persons who want to gain a substantial advantage in terms of reduced assessments on capital gains, and annual income, as well as on their personal estate at the time of their death. The charitable remainder trusts provided a unique opportunity for these persons.

There are two types of trust agreements utilized by those interested in establishing the charitable remainder trust.

First, the unitrust. The unitrust may be established by a donor providing a constant rate of return during the duration of the trust. The donor determines the annual percentage of return on the trust. The return must equal, or exceed, 5 percent per year. It may be designated for one, or more, individuals, and the yield may be designated in a skip-generation manner, that is, inclusive of donors and grandchildren. Funds may be added to the trust periodically.

The percentage of yield will remain constant regardless of the size of the sums in trust.

As the sums in trust increase in value, the distribution of revenue, based on a fixed percentage rate, will increase. Likewise, as the sums in the trust decrease in value, the distribution will also decrease. Those benefiting from the annual payments from the trust can only be certain that the percentage of income will remain constant.

Second, the annuity trust. The annuity trust may be established by a donor providing a constant annual return during the duration of the trust. The donor determines the percentage of return to be gained from the trust annually based on the size of funds used to establish the trust initially. It must equal, or exceed, 5 percent based on the funds placed in trust. The annual distribution to beneficiaries may be designated for one, or more, individuals, and the yield may be designated in a skip-generation manner, that is, inclusive of donors and grandchildren.

Funds may not be added to the trust. Since fixed amount from the trust, and/or earnings of the trust, is distributed, the principal contributed for the trust must be respected as the sum in trust that governs distributions annually.

As the sums in trust increase in value, the distribution remains a fixed sum, and the growth may result in the benefit to the charity as remainder. As the sums in the trust decrease in value, the distribution, at a fixed annual sum, may decrease the principal value of the trust as capital is required to pay the annuity. In this event the charity, as remainderman, may receive a lesser amount than was contributed to establish the trust initially. Those benefiting from the trust can be certain that their annual income will remain constant.

Those benefiting from the trust can be certain that their annual income will remain constant.

There are four types of donors with primary interests in the unitrust or the annuity trust:

1. The philanthropically inclined individual who is anxious to establish a substantial income for his or her spouse and children or grandchildren over an extended period of time with the ultimate benefit sustaining the ministry and mission of the local church or some other eleemosynary organization.

2. The philanthropically inclined individual who seeks to avoid tax on capital gains of real estate or personal property and, at the same time, provide for the annual needs of family members or friends over an extended period of time with the ultimate benefit sustaining the ministry and mission of the local church or some other eleemosynary organization.

3. The philanthropically inclined individual who seeks to avoid tax on capital gains from investments and/or business interests and, at the same time, provide for the annual needs of family members or friends over an extended period of time with the ultimate benefit sustaining the ministry and mission of his church or some other eleemosynary organization.

4. The philanthropically inclined individual who, as a result of advanced age or deteriorating health wants to place his or her assets in trust to secure an annual income and provide for the needs of spouse and family members over an extended period of time with the ultimate benefit sustaining the ministry and mission of the local church or some other eleemosynary organization.

In serving persons with these philanthropic interests it is not in the best interest of the donor, or the local church, for the task force to serve as trustee or suggest that the institution serve as trustee or manage the trust. In the connectional system, denominations have established foundations to serve individuals in this process with modest fees for administering the trust. At the expiration of the trust, the remainder goes to the designated organization. For others, the trust departments of local banking institutions are readily available to provide the same service, and while the administration fee will tend to be higher than that required by the denominational trust as a nonprofit organization, the services will be in the best interest of both the donor and the organization.

In many cases the donor may have a preference. The donor may not make a final decision or share in the administration of the trust. The task force should be prepared to make recommendation relative to the administration of the trust to the official board or trustees of the institution in the event this decision falls to the agency.

Based on the principle that an informed people will do the right thing, it is expedient that descriptive brochures be available to the members and friends of the local church or organization listing the names of those persons serving on the Charitable Remainder Trust Task Force. The descriptive brochure should provide information concerning both the unitrust and annuity trust and include examples showing how this philanthropic instrument may be used advantageously by both the donor and the institution.

From time to time the task force will want to include in bulletins and newsletters brief pieces explaining the charitable remainder trust as well as illustrations of the type of donor that would be interested in this type opportunity.

When a trust is established, considerable publicity should be given to the matter even if the names of the donors, those benefiting from the trust, and the sum placed in trust are not included in the release. As in other philanthropic procedures, news of this type tends to have a domino effect, and others will respond to the opportunity as they learn of the advantages to donors, beneficiaries, and the organization itself.

It is appropriate for task forces to introduce the charitable remainder trust opportunities in seminars and workshops. Those serving as staff persons on a denominational foundation, as well as trust officers in banking institutions, are able and willing to share in such events.

The task force should be able to guide individual prospective donors to the institutional representatives who can serve as the administrators of a trust and to qualified legal counselors who will serve the best interests of both the donor and the institution as the donor gains understanding and proceeds in the decision-making process.

Approximately 5 percent of the members of a church or organization will provide potential for this instrument for philanthropic giving.

18

Selecting Members for the Charitable Remainder Trust Task Force

Because those considering the establishment of a charitable remainder trust will generally be persons of substantial means, it is important that the members of the Charitable Remainder Trust Task Force be qualified to meet with the prospective donor from a position of strong financial integrity. Under no condition should the members' occupations create a conflict of interest in serving the prospective donor or the institution.

Here are several keys to enlisting the right types of persons to serve on the Charitable Remainder Trust Task Force.

First, it would be well if one member of the task force held an administrative role in a corporation or a successful small business and was respected by peers as a decision maker.

This person need not have great wealth or be involved directly in the charitable remainder trust either as a donor or recipient. Certainly the person should be known for his or her interests in philanthropic giving and the long-term economic well-being of the organization.

Second, another member of the task force should be an educator. Throughout the discussion of the various task forces I have emphasized two things: Philanthropic giving will result from an educational process, and an informed people will do the right thing. Obviously, many who work in the field of education will not have sufficient economic worth to consider a charitable trust. They are, however, capable of explaining procedures, requirements, and the means whereby the interests and needs of both the donor and organization may be met through a charitable remainder trust. Persons of considerable means will have no reservation approaching an educator for information if the person is identified as a member of the task force.

Third, a person who is employed in a banking firm or investment organization would round out the task force. One who is consistently relied upon in areas of fiscal integrity and financial credibility. The person should be trusted with financial resources and considered competent in financial matters. This type is an excellent source for seeking counsel in appraisals, relating to both real estate and personal property and for market analysis of resources that may be considered as instruments for funding the charitable remainder trust.

Those in the field of finance will have ready access to those who can be recruited for seminars and workshops on philanthropic giving. The interrelationship of vocational interests and concerns among persons of this type make for an excellent reservoir of expertise for the local church as it seeks to develop new understandings in philanthropic processes and opportunities.

19

The Task Force on Grantsmanship

A sizable portion of the philanthropic dollars available to humanitarian and life-enrichment services in the United States results from grants. There are over twenty thousand foundations and fifty thousand corporations and denominational, ecumenical, and community sources from which funds are available, ranging from sums as modest as $100 dollars to sums as large as millions of dollars. Many provide potential for funding to the local church.

Obviously, in reviewing grants indices few sources contribute to religion, and one will have difficulty finding evidence of substantial funding to a local church unless it relates to the restoration of the facility as a historical landmark. Yet, in completing a comprehensive search, one will find that a reasonably large percentage of the funding goes to programs either established by a local church or under the auspices of a local congregation.

It is essential, therefore, that the local church establish a vehicle for overturing and administering grants. The First United Methodist Church in Hollis, New York has established the Hollis Center for Community Service; the First United Presbyterian Church in Salem, Ohio has established The Good Samaritan Fund; the Littleton United Methodist Church in Littleton, Colorado has established The Foundation for the Fine Arts; and the Community Church of Woodland Hills, California has established West Valley Community Service. In no case has the funding instrument been established as a separate corporation. Each, however, is served by a grants task force, and each is under the auspices of the local church.

Establishing the vehicle for overturing and administering grants makes it easier for a funding source to contribute to an organization that is neither sectarian nor "religious." The fact that the organization is under the auspices of a local church provides the credibility that a funding source will welcome. Few grants will come to a local church without such an instrumentality.

Now it must be understood that grants available to the local church will be those that strengthen the community service and outreach of a local parish. With few exceptions, they will not be available for either the sacramental or the liturgical rites. These responsibilities duly belong to the members of the parish. But those services provided by, or under the auspices of, a local church that are indeed community service and life-enrichment programs will receive funding in many cases.

Illustrations in those categories would include a grant for a parish kitchen to feed the homeless or the poor in a limited geographical area; rest rooms, ramps, and elevators that would enable physically handicapped or aged persons to share in appropriate community programs in the local church facility; staff members to serve in the areas of counseling, vocational rehabilitation, and community service orchestration; and seed money for developing preschool, latchkey, and senior citizens programs.

No funding source is likely to provide resources for the total program or improvements, but most will fund a considerable portion. And, if true cost accounting is exercised in the process, one will discover that regardless of the funding need the local church or institution is putting considerable money into the particular project in terms of facilities, staff time, and administrative costs. Therefore, in establishing the budget for the project it is essential that a comprehensive cost accounting be made in order to arrive at a fair representation of the organization's contribution. The funding need will then be those funds not available to the project except through a grant. In most cases this cost will represent between 40 and 60 percent of the budget for the project.

In presenting the opportunity to a funding source a proposal should be developed to include the following:

1. Title—one sentence
2. Purpose—one paragraph
3. Description—limit to five paragraphs
4. Progress—one paragraph
5. Budget—not to exceed ten items
6. Funding need—one sentence
7. Signature—name, address, telephone number, and position held by the signer in relation to the project (chairperson, administrator, coordinator, etc.)

When the proposal is finished, a comprehensive search should be made to find as many as ten funding sources that will consider the proposal favorably. In each event the proposal, individually typed, should be sent with a covering letter to each funding source. Xerox copies of the proposal should be provided only in those cases where a funding source requires more than one copy.

No local church should develop projects or programs just to get grants. In developing ministry and mission there will be many areas for which grants may be available to assist in funding.

A nonprofit agency serving denominations, judicatories, and local churches and their related organizations in this area is The National Consultation on Financial Development, 31 Langerfeld Road, Hillsdale, New Jersey 07642 (201-644-8890). The service may be provided on a contractual, per diem, or piece work basis. If a local church asks the organization to prepare a proposal, the cost will be $225. Whether or not the organization prepares the proposal, they will make a funding-source search and provide the ten most likely foundations to fund the particular project or program. The fee is $150. I know of no other organization providing this service.

While community services are a means of evangelical outreach, they are also the means of local church redemption in many cases. I could sight case after case where the local parish actually came alive as a result of a program it has developed, and for which funding has been secured, that has resulted in the constitution of a vibrant and vital congregational life.

20

Selecting Members for the Grantsmanship Task Force

It would be good if the responsibilities of the Grantsmanship Task Force were to be confined to merely writing proposals, completing funding searches, and mailing the overtures to funding sources. However, in most cases the task force will face these responsibilities

1. Conceptualizing projects for foundation, corporation, and organizational funding
2. Estimating and projecting costs for the program or project over a period of time
3. Determining what percentage of the cost may be requested from a funding source.
4. Writing the proposal
5. Completing a funding search to determine which funding sources to ask

In many cases a task force can handle the first three steps. The other two are usually contracted to an individual or agency that has expertise in the area.

As funding will be available for community service and life-enriching programs, I would look for a person who is well informed concerning opportunities available to all types of individuals in the local church and those particular needs that are not adequately met to serve as the first member of the task force. This person may well be a social worker, an administrator in a social service agency, or a person relating to community service from a chamber of commerce or association for commerce and industry.

A second person may well be an individual who relates directly to a particular area of community service either in terms of vocation, avocation, interest, or personal involvement. A case in point may be a parent of a preschool child, a relative of a handicapped person, or a senior citizen. While it is likely that there will be a tendency for this person to conceptualize programs and opportunities from his or her own vantage point, some will have the ability to see beyond their particular area of interest and concern to other needs.

It is essential that one person serving on the task force be directly involved in the administrative processes of the local parish in terms of program development and the long-range policies of the institution. This may be the layperson holding the highest elective post in the parish, a member of the governing board, or the presiding officer in a program of the institution. Examples include the clerk of session in a Presbyterian Church, the senior warden in an Episcopal church, the lay leader in a United Methodist church; a Sunday school superintendent, president of a women's association, chairperson for a board of trustees.

While many persons may be enlisted to provide ideas, experience, documentation, and needs in order that the task force fulfill its purpose, it is in the best interests or the organization, again, if the task force is limited to three members.

21

Financial Administration Task Force

There are few organizations that have been as poor stewards of their financial resources as has the local church. Throughout my pastoral ministry, which has spanned over a third of a century, I recall many times officers speaking well of a bank's services because "they give us free checking." On one occasion I discovered twenty-seven checking and savings accounts among the treasury, the organizations, and the Sunday school classes of a local church. In an eight year period the funds in those accounts had not been less than thirty thousand dollars at any particular time. Only $500 held by a sewing circle was in a passbook account drawing simple interest! I have seen this again and again and again!

Each local church must be a responsible steward of their financial resources. Every dollar should be working to develop resources for ministry and mission when not expended directly for ministry and mission. This will require two things: 1. The consolidation of the banking procedures in the local church, and 2. investment procedures whereby the organization may take full advantage of the earning potential for funding in a comprehensive investment portfolio ranging from Now accounts to long-term certificates of deposit as allowed by the cash flow needs, and projected income, of the organization.

The financial secretary of a Methodist church in New Jersey told of her personal involvement in investing building funds in the parish over a period of three years, which resulted in earnings of more than thirty thousand dollars! Yet, this concern and interest was limited to a single fund in that parish.

How may the two objectives mentioned above be attained?

The first (central management of accounts) may be attained by incorporating all of the funds of the various treasuries and organizations in a single accounting procedure. This will not eliminate the numerous accounts. Actually, the central treasury will become a "bank," and accounting will be provided for each of the organizations having funds on deposit. Instead of individual treasurers writing checks, they write a warrant that instructs the central treasurer to issue a check and to debit their account in the accounting process.

The second (comprehensive investment of funds) may be attained by projecting cash flow in terms of income and expenditures and determining the minimum balance that is required by the organization. This should be in a checking account drawing interest. Further study will reveal which funds may be deposited in longer term investment opportunities, namely, from thirty days to four years or more.

The local churches engaged in investments usually agree on one of two courses in distributing the earnings.

Many organizations choose to designate the earnings as accruing to the parent body for capital funding needs. Others will distribute the earnings quarterly, based on the balance of funds in the particular accounts on a fixed date in each quarter. A task force might use the third Friday of the third week in the third month of each quarter as the date for distribution.

A local church cannot continuously emphasize the importance of personal estate planning and the significance of Christian stewardship on an individual basis if the organization itself is not providing an example of sound fiscal procedures in exercising stewardship over its resources.

22

Selecting Members for the Task Force for Financial Administration

The first person I would consider to serve on the Task Force for Financial Administration would be a person who works in commerce, industry, or an organizational structure and has management skills, that is, can orchestrate departments and divisions and consolidate procedures and efforts in attaining objectives. This person may be a company president, a plant manager, the executive in a large corporation, or an administration officer in a community service agency.

This person must be capable of meeting with people, explaining the importance of cooperating in the larger scheme of things, and assuring those with reservations of the integrity of the process. Those management and communication skills work for General Motors, and they will serve the best interests of the local church.

The second person I would want on the task force is an individual who is well versed in accounting procedures—education, vocation, or interests. The person should understand ledgers, budgets, budgeting procedures, expenditures, and bookkeeping processes. This person may be employed as a certified public accountant, an accountant, a bookkeeper, or an auditor. In no case should a person employed by the local church or agency serve on the Task Force for Financial Administration, although another task force may not present a conflict for an employee.

The third person should be one who is vocationally, or avocationally, knowledgeable in the field of investments not from the standpoint of stocks and bonds but from the standpoint of reasonable earnings from sound investment procedures.

Remember, in selecting these members for the task force consider their responsibilities confined to financial administration and not to investment of capital funding in terms of endowments and trusts. These would fall into an entirely different area and are not a subject in this book.

The third person may be one schooled in the banking industry or work in banking or as an investment counselor.

Each person will bring their strengths to the task force, and the administration and operation of the procedures will be appreciated by every member, and applauded by every organization involved, as they see their money working for the extension of ministry and mission in the local church.

23

The Cabinet

After reviewing the numerous task forces and the types of persons recommended for each, it is only natural that one raise the question, How do we put it all together?

A local church cannot have a half-dozen or more task forces going in a half-dozen directions, and the organization cannot endure a half-dozen overtures for funding being thrown at them at one time. It is essential that task forces work in concert, making their contributions and exercising their responsibilities at a time when they can be most effective in serving members and friends as prospective donors.

It would be well then if each task force was represented on a cabinet that would consist of one member from each task force and a chairperson, or presiding officer, who would be elected by the cabinet to serve for a period of not more than three years.

The cabinet would meet three responsibilities.

First, meetings of the cabinet would provide opportunity for each task force to submit a report of their activities and objectives. It is important that each task force know what the other task forces are doing in order that they not compete with but complement the services of the other task forces.

Second, the cabinet would monitor the procedures for the work of the various task forces and determine the time schedule for particular activities and functions in order that each may have the advantage of the best timing for serving the common good.

Third, the cabinet would orchestrate the projects and activities of the various task forces as an integral part of the institution and strengthen the witness of each task force in conducting their service, and attaining their objective, as a vital part of the overall stewardship enlistment and commitment process.

The cabinet should meet monthly, and this body should be the instrument through which the task forces report to, or seek approval from, the administrative board of the local church or agency. The recommendations of the task forces (always as reports) are passed on to the administrative board through the cabinet, and responses flow back to the task forces through the cabinet.

The task forces will not function effectively and the procedure will not proceed well over the course of years if each task force works directly with the administrative board. The time would prove unwieldly, and the number of task forces would be reduced substantially over a period of a very short time.

The cabinet is the key to orchestrating and administrating the services of the task forces for enlistment and commitment in the local church.

Index